The Happy Home Project*

Copyright © 2011
Hachette Filipacchi Media U.S., Inc.

First published in 2011 in the United States of America
by Filipacchi Publishing
1271 Avenue of the Americas
New York, NY 10020

Woman's Day is a registered trademark of Hachette Filipacchi Media U.S., Inc.

Design: D'Mello+Felmus Design Inc. (www.dmellofelmus.com)

Editor: Lauren Kuczala

Production: Lynn Scaglione and Annie Andres

ISBN-13: 978-1-936297-48-1

Library of Congress control number: 2010940287

Printed in China

photo credits

Cover: courtesy of **Hickory Chair**; Page 4: **Aimée Herring**; p. 8: courtesy of **Hickory Chair**; p. 10, 11: **Karyn Millet**; p. 12–13: **Paul Whicheloe**; p. 14, 15: **Gridley & Graves**; p. 16, 17: courtesy of **Benjamin Moore**; p. 18: **Paul Whicheloe**; p. 19: courtesy of **Benjamin Moore**; p. 20, 21: courtesy of **York**; p. 23: **Paul Whicheloe**; p. 24: **Gordon Beall**; p. 27, top: **Edmund Barr**; p. 27, bottom: **Stacey Brandford**; p. 28: **Virginia McDonald**; p. 29: **Ed Gorlich**; p. 30, 33, 34, 35: **David Papazian**; p. 37: courtesy of **Wood-Mode**; p. 37: courtesy of **York**; p. 38: **Aimée Herring**; p. 41: courtesy of **Carlisle**; p. 42: **Gridley & Graves**; p. 45: **James Yochum**; p. 46, left: **Jamie Hadley**; p. 46, right: **Karen Melvin**; p. 47: **Rob Karosis**; p. 49: **Lauren Rubenstein**; p. 51: courtesy of **Century Furniture**; p. 52–53: courtesy of **C.R. Laine**; p. 54: courtesy of **Kincaid Furniture**; p. 56: **Kelly Quin**; p. 57: **Jason Madara**; p. 58: **Gridley & Graves**; p. 61, 62: **Jason Madara**; p. 63: **Nancy Hill**; p. 64: **Paul Whicheloe**; p. 66: **Gordon Beall**; p. 69: **Aimée Herring**; p. 71: courtesy of **Hickory Chair**; p. 72, 73: **Aimée Herring**; p. 76: **Paul Whicheloe**; p. 79: **James Yochum**; p. 80, left: **Keith Scott Morton**; p. 80, right: **Emily Jenkins Followill**; p. 83: **Paul Whicheloe**; p. 84: **Jamie Hadley**; p. 86–87: **Kip Dawkins**; p. 88: **John Gould Bessler**; p. 90: **Jason Madara**; p. 92: **Aimée Herring**; p. 93, 95: **James Yochum**; p. 96, 97: **Kip Dawkins**; p. 98–99: courtesy of **Thermador**; p. 100, 101, 102, 103: **James Yochum**; p. 104, 105: courtesy of **Hickory Chair**; p. 107: **Liz Glasgow**; p. 108: courtesy of **Serena & Lily**; p. 109: **Maura McEvoy**/courtesy of **Garnet Hill**; p. 110–111, 112, 103 top: **Keith Scott Morton**; p. 103, bottom: **James Yochum**; p. 115: **Paul Whicheloe**; p. 116, 119: **John Merkl**; p. 120, 121, 122, 123: **James Yochum**; p. 124, 125, 126, 127: **Gridley & Graves**; p. 128, 12–9, 130, 131: **James Yochum**; p. 132-133, 134, 135: **Kimberly Gavin**; p. 136, 137, 138, 139: **Paul Whicheloe**; p. 140, 141: **Aimée Herring**; p. 142, 143: **Grey Crawford**; p. 146: **Kate Sears**; p. 148, 149, 150, 151: **Gridley & Graves**; p. 152–153, 154, 155: **Jeff McNamara**; p. 156–157, 158, 159 bottom left and bottom right: **John Gruen**; p. 159, top right: **Kate Sears**.

Woman'sDay

The Happy Home Project*

*** A Practical Guide to Adding
Style and Substance to Your Home**

by Jean Nayar

filipacchi
publishing

contents

Who doesn't want a happy home?

When I began writing this book, my home was already happy. In fact, over the years when I was working in an office building, I would often come home at the end of the day, walk through the front door and whisper gratefully to myself, "I live in heaven."

An imperfect heaven, to be sure. But heaven nonetheless. Still, I had dreams—and many of them revolved around my home. Others had to do with my career. So I set out on a journey to see if I could make some of the dreams in both of these areas come true. And with the support of my husband, Anil; my editor and publisher, Dorothée Walliser; and my fantastic family and friends, I embarked on *The Happy Home Project*.

It began last April and was inspired by a book called *The Happiness Project*, which was written by Gretchen Rubin and supported by *Woman's Day* magazine. Knowing the time was right, I endeavored to take on a similar project, and launched a blog where I could chronicle my experiences and findings. My project, however, was targeted specifically on the makings of a happy home, where my experience lies. And I started with an ambitious wish list of home improvements, which I aimed to take on in my own home over the course of a year. In the process, I also planned to explore a wide range of cross-cultural design ideas, take them for a test drive in my own domain and report on the results. Though the journey is incomplete, much of what I learned and encountered along the way is contained within the pages of this book.

At the height of the chaos and upheaval caused by the renovation projects in our home, I was writing the chapter in this book called Spirit (hilarious, I'm sure, to the gods of irony who surely orchestrated the timing). Not surprisingly, with so many people coming and going and so much daily commotion—multiple deliveries, endless appointments, mountains of tools and plaster and floor tiles and cabinet boxes and door handles and paint cans and debris-filled garbage bags and Lord knows what else—this was also the time when mistakes were sometimes made, budgets were overrun, tempers occasionally flared, and—in the quiet moments after the workers left but before my husband came home—tears were sometimes shed. It wasn't so much about the stress of the reconstruction, I came to realize, as it was about the change in my life in general—and much of it seemed to be just beyond the grasp of my control. My home really was a reflection of the change that was happening within me. And it was more change than I was really ready for.

Eventually, though, the calm followed the storm, and I was able to fulfill half of the wishes on my wish list. But not without heaps of help from my family and friends. In fact, as I pressed along on this journey, dozens of new friendships bloomed. And I'm especially grateful to all of the design industry friends who sponsored or supported my efforts.

While I wouldn't recommend writing a book in the midst of a multilevel home improvement project, doing so was enlightening on many levels. No one ever said life is always serene. Chicken soup is one thing, but a healthy challenge can be good for the soul, too. So frayed nerves and depleted bank account aside, I'm glad to have had the opportunity—and the support I needed—to take on this project. For the process has enriched my home—and my life—substantially. And by sharing some of the lessons learned, I hope the ideas contained in this book may brighten the way for your own endeavors.

As I write these words after completing the book, I look toward a future that is wide open and entirely uncertain, but one thing is crystal clear—my closets are organized and beautiful, my walls are freshly painted and my renovated kitchen makes me really happy. Of course the material comforts, in my case, are simply the icing on the cake, for they're just a dim reflection of my real joy, which is the beauty of my simple life and the numerous and astoundingly wonderful people who fill it. Yet, mine isn't the only story with a happy ending (or, I should say, middle) in this book. Every single home and every single room on the pages that follow has a story, a message or an idea that can be of service to anyone on the road toward domestic bliss. I hope these stories will inspire you to embark on your own happy home project—and if you come through a changed person like I have, my bet is that it will be for the better.

ingredients of a happy home

Surely there's no one-size-fits-all recipe for a happy home. But after doing lots of research, taking lots of test drives, and making lots of trials and lots of errors, I've come up with a list of ingredients that I'm convinced contribute to the joy in mine. By sharing these ingredients, I hope you'll try mixing a dash of one here with a dollop of another there, combining them with your personal alchemy to see what effect they have on the happiness of your own home. Here are my ingredients:

Access to nature Nothing brightens a home like a touch of Mother Nature, whether it's a burst of fresh air, a ray of sunshine, a lakeside view or a tiny potted plant. A connection with nature reminds you that you're a part of a larger order that has rhythms and energy and laws that reflect and nourish the microcosm that is you.

Just-right spaces More than not-too-big and not-too-small, just-right spaces contain just enough stuff to make them comfortable, functional and visually appealing to you. Just-right rooms are well edited and include only things that have meaning or a purpose. They usually don't happen overnight, but rather evolve slowly over time as you eliminate and add just-right things as you go along.

Something for everyone When a home accommodates more than one person, it needs to feel like home to everyone who lives in it. Allocating nooks and crannies to different forms of personal expression can allow disparate tastes to happily coexist in a patchwork that provides room for all.

Personality If there's one thing that puts a damper on happiness in a home, it's cookie-cutter rooms. Happy rooms show something of the personality of their owners, whether it's a collection of vintage quilts, a gutsy work of art, a handmade throw or a favorite color.

Elements of comfort To many of us, the word *comfort*—as it relates to the home—connotes overstuffed chairs, fluffy pillows and fuzzy throws. But in this context, elements of comfort have more to do with an individual's sense of beauty and the objects and colors and shapes that put him or her at ease.

Order An ordered home isn't just about having a place for everything with everything in its place. It's about all of the elements—and the rituals they support—that ease the flow from dusk to dawn, spring to fall, work to play. It's also about eliminating the inconsequential and celebrating the essential. As a landscape designer I know says, "More of less is always a good thing."

Private zones In his classic work *The Poetics of Space*, the philosopher Gaston Bachelard argued that the chief role of a home is to serve as a place for daydreaming. Private spaces, whether a room of one's own, a window seat or a corner in a garden, let intimate dreams unfold.

The element of surprise. A surprising element in a home can take on all kinds of guises. It might be a whimsical pop of color, a mysterious garden path or a witty work of art—anything that shifts the energy of a space and engages the imagination.

Carbon-footprint consciousness An eco-friendly home will not only make you happier because you're being a good global citizen, it'll make you, your family and the planet healthier. And it can save you money over the long haul, too.

A sense of spirit Spirit in the home is about a connection to something beyond the material things that define and fill it. It might be a sense of kinship with the imagination of the people who made the furniture or art in your home. It might be a feeling of community that occurs in a home that's shared with friends and family. Or it might be a sacred sensibility symbolized by a fountain, a statue, a stone or other emblem that represents your view of the divine.

—*Jean Nayar*

Note: As I finished writing this book, I managed to accomplish about half of the 20 projects on my wish list. To see the complete list, visit my blog, TheHappyHomeWorkshop.com, where you'll find posts on my experiences along with reporting on design industry news in general.

style

a well-crafted home is much more than the sum of its parts—its rooms, stairways, chairs, tables, tiles and curtains. It's a unified ensemble that reflects your personality, nurtures your spirit and supports how you live. Viewed as integral elements in a grander scheme, the individual pieces of a house become like notes in a musical composition—each playing a vital role in the overall harmony. Establishing a clear sense of style will help you choose furnishings, materials and colors to shape a home that makes you happy.

Clarifying your sense of style before you embark on renovating a house or decorating a room will also ease the process of shaping spaces over time. Fortunately, once you've identified and embraced your style, you can also adapt it as you go along without necessarily starting over. When you're clear about your style as a reflection of your tastes and values, it's easier to fine-tune it as you evolve and grow or as your needs change.

The pages that follow highlight a few livable styles—traditional, modern, country, global-influenced—that will stand the test of time. Yet each section includes ideas that will allow these styles to remain fluid and fresh. By identifying the elements that resonate with you, you can establish a foundation of forms and a palette of materials and colors that will help you create spaces that feel natural. And by remaining open to shapes and colors outside your comfort zone, you can create spaces that reflect not only who you are but also who you want to become.

How a room looks is one thing, but how it lives is another. In order to shape a home that will, in turn, positively shape you, you'll also need to take a look at how you and your family live and what you need to make your day-to-day activities run smoothly. You may also assess how to gradually introduce ingredients that can help you turn your home into a haven on a timetable that works for your budget and circumstances.

If you want to create rooms that are truly satisfying, flexibility and a long view should be part of your plan from the start—they'll allow you to make your investments wisely. If you start with a baseline of the best quality furnishings and finishes you can afford, you'll have a firm foundation to build upon. As your tastes change and your budget grows, you can layer in extras that enhance the quality of your life or reflect subtle shifts in your aesthetic point of view.

fresh traditional

If you're drawn to historic formal houses, then odds are you're attracted to traditional furnishings and materials, too. Maybe you live in a house that's luxurious and refined, with formal spaces rooted in European styles of the past. Or maybe you live in a Colonial- or Greek Revival–style house that's more modest in scale and architectural ornamentation. You may even live in a new structure that incorporates characteristics of historic styles. In any of these cases, these are typical features in traditional-style homes:

Architecture and finishes: Rooms with symmetrical features and layouts with elements like crown moldings, divided-light windows, wood floors and mahogany or painted wainscoting are common characteristics of traditional environments.

Furnishings: European or American antiques, such as Sheraton, Louis XVI, Regency, Chippendale or Queen Anne pieces, are typical of rooms with a traditional style. Newer variations of these furnishings, such as updated Windsor chairs or four-poster beds made of walnut or mahogany also appear in traditional-style homes. Upholstered pieces might include sofas with camelbacks, wing chairs, or chairs with rolled arms and skirts or turned wooden legs.

Fabrics and soft furnishings: Silks, linens, velvets or wools with woven patterns, such as stripes and damasks prevail in traditional rooms. Full-length draperies, sometimes topped with valances or pelmets, usually frame the windows. Slipcovers are tailored to fit dining chairs and upholstered seating and often include full-length pleated skirts and piping of other trims. Bedding may include tailored dust ruffles.

A tailored English-style leather settee offsets contemporary art and a mid-20th-century daybed and chair by Hans Wegner in the living room of this home. Floor-to-ceiling ivory cotton curtains and an Asian carpet soften the crisp lines of the double-height room.

Colors: Traditional settings usually include familiar colors, including deep reds, soothing olive or sage greens, and quiet tans, taupe, khaki, creams and other neutrals. Sometimes, though, they'll include bolder historical colors, such as bright yellow or Tiffany blue, or feature tone-on-tone schemes. Departing slightly from any of these colors—using berry red instead of burgundy, for instance—can be a simple way to freshen the look of a traditional room over time.

Landscape: Outside, a traditional home might be surrounded by manicured gardens and the lawn might include garden structures such as a pergola, an arbor or a gazebo. Alternatively, the trees and shrubs might be more naturalistic, like those in an 18th-century English garden.

⊙ *Elements That Keep the Look Fresh*
Updated wing chair • Modern table or lamp • Lively colors

soft modern

Those who favor a soft modern style might be as drawn to a house designed in the mid-20th century as they are to a condo designed in the early 21st century. Lovers of modern furniture often successfully freshen traditional-style houses with contemporary pieces, too. It's all in the mix. Hallmarks of the style are clean lines, few decorative flourishes and asymmetry. Other common features of the style include the following.

Architecture and finishes: Settings with open spaces that flow into each other, asymmetrical spatial arrangements, large windows with unimpeded views and a decided lack of architectural ornamentation will put modernists at ease.

Furnishings: For modernists who regard their home as a sanctuary, rooms might be understated oases of comfort and calm with subtle neutral palettes, natural fabrics and a carefully edited mix of clean-lined Italian- or Danish-designed furnishings. A large flat-screen TV may be the focal point of the family room, where a crisp sofa or sectional upholstered in leather will likely serve as the dominant piece of furniture. A kitchen might feature an eco-conscious engineered quartz countertop or reclaimed wood or bamboo floors. A simple platform bed, topped with undyed organic bedding (or, alternatively, a graphic geometric print), would likely be the centerpiece of a soft modern bedroom. In lieu of the metal and resin pieces likely to be found in cool modern rooms, furnishings in soft modern rooms are more often made of wood.

easy country

Country style is all about comfort. A country home might be a seaside beach house, a gentleman's farmhouse or a lakeside cottage. While some country houses are quite sophisticated and grand, many are compact and modest. Whether old or new, large or small, country houses are often characterized by the following qualities:

Architecture and finishes: Country dwellings are typically compact, one-story structures. The walls of their rooms are often covered with bead board, board-and-batten paneling, or wainscoting, which is frequently painted white. Wide-plank pine wood floors are common in casual country homes, and sometimes the wood floors are painted or stenciled. Oak floors prevail in more sophisticated country houses.

Furnishings: In a country home, furnishings might include family heirlooms or hand-me-downs mixed with flea-market finds. Wood furnishings are often painted—white, red, pale blue, yellow or green. Overstuffed sofas and flea-market chairs encourage a relaxed ambience, and upholstered furniture is sometimes topped with slipcovers to unify disparate pieces or minimize maintenance. Dining rooms often include a farm table, wooden chairs or benches, and a weathered hutch or sideboard.

Fabrics and soft furnishings: Cushions, curtains and bedding in floral, gingham and striped cotton fabrics predominate in a country home. Swedish checks and ticking stripes or French provincial toiles or paisleys are also common. Bedrooms are pretty, with painted metal beds and handmade quilts. And wood floors are often topped with boldly striped flat-weave or natural jute or sisal rugs. New takes on these patterns will enliven the look.

Colors: Wall colors in country houses tend toward pastels—pale blue, pink, green, yellow—usually offset by crisp white molding. Stronger paint colors—apple green or tomato red—can bring fresh energy to country-style rooms.

Landscape: Outdoors, a country house is often surrounded by a picket fence. A swing on a covered porch is also common, as are stone or wooden benches and a potting shed in the yard. Border gardens often brim with plump hydrangeas, and the landscape might feature an arbor or trellis covered with climbing roses.

Fabrics and soft furnishings: Cool modernists often avoid soft furnishings like curtains and shades, especially those made of fabrics with strong or feminine patterns, and instead generally leave windows bare or cover them simply with scrim shades or roller blinds. But soft modernists are likely to embrace simple soft furnishings, like unfussy curtains or Roman shades, to bring warmth to the style without infringing on the clutter-free look they favor. However, the fabrics they choose for these elements are often made of neutral cotton, linen, felt or wools with rich textures and limited patterns.

Colors: In modern houses, colors can run the gamut from the palest and most predictable neutrals to the boldest and most surprising brights. In general, contrast is key, with cooler modernists opting for black and white and warm modernists choosing grays, browns and creams. Sometimes an accent wall in a bold or strong color, such as turquoise or orange, will serve as a focal point in a spare modern room.

Landscape: Modern houses are often designed to harmonize with their settings, fitting in with the landscape like hand in glove. Their surroundings are often naturalistic and peppered with monolithic stone benches and wrap-around terraces, enabling their inhabitants to commune with nature. A trickling fountain may sit at one side of a patio and a simple Japanese-inspired pool house might sit at the end of a placid pool. Gardens might feature crisply clipped parterres or be punctuated with low-maintenance succulents.

⊙ *Elements That Soften Modern Rooms*
Textured throws • Asian carpets • A wooden antique • Crisp curtains

⊙ *Elements That Add Dimension to the Look*
Rattan drum tables • Modern lamps and picture frames • Fresh fabrics

Left and opposite: A Moroccan leather pouf and, ethnic baskets and objets d'art and a mix of contemporary and traditional furnishings bring eclectic flavor to a traditional room. A unique color scheme, including Benjamin Moore's Vintage Wine on the ceiling and wall in the coat cubby, and Etruscan and Wasabi on the walls, adds spice to the mix.

global-influenced

The home interiors of adventurous travelers usually reflect their globetrotting inclinations and are often infused with furnishings and accents acquired along the course of their journeys. People with global-influenced style generally aren't driven by trends, yet they often set them. A global-influenced home could be anywhere from the city to exurbia, in the mountains or near the sea. Here's a summary of the elements you're likely to see in rooms defined by this style:

Architecture and finishes: The architecture of homes with a global influence is generally rooted in the style of the region in which the home is located. Colonial influences, such as dark-stained wooden beams, wide-plank wood floors and creamy plaster walls, are also common elements of the backdrop.

Furnishings: Living spaces may include an offbeat mix of furnishings—mid-century Scandinavian modern chairs, a Moroccan pouf, an African wooden stool. Spaces may include a mix of modern and antique furniture, or they might be styled with a commingling of contemporary furniture and Indian, African or Chinese handicrafts. Accents from around the globe may infuse private spaces with international flavor, too.

Fabrics and soft furnishings: Saris used as canopies, batik pillows, cushions covered with African kente cloth and Asian rugs are all likely soft touches in global-influenced spaces.

Colors: Global-inspired eclectic rooms may feature neutral backdrops with rich or vibrant accents or include intense, offbeat hues on the walls.

Landscape: You might find outside a string of Chinese lanterns over a teak table on a terrace, or Spanish wrought-iron cocktail tables and Moroccan pierced-metal lanterns on a patio.

⊙ *Elements That Keep the Style Cohesive*
Neutral upholstery fabrics • Consistent color scheme • Oil-rubbed bronze or cast-iron fixtures

color and pattern

The colors in a room are as essential to its style as the architectural elements, furnishings and fabrics. Selecting colors for your home can be one of the most exciting parts of the decorating process. It can also be one of the most intimidating. While most of us know instinctively which colors we like and which we don't, choosing just the right shade of any given hue and mixing it with other colors in a room can be overwhelming, as the options are virtually limitless.

To take the stress out of selecting a wall color, paint companies often come up with cohesive palette collections to help consumers choose colors without fear. These color groupings often include contrasting or complementary colors that harmonize in tone and value—and they can be enormously helpful in minimizing the time you'll need to spend testing different shades on a wall. That said, following a prescriptive approach to color keeps you from creating personal spaces that truly reflect your own tastes and values. It's important to trust your instincts. There's a reason why you like what you like—and surrounding yourself with hues that please you will put you at ease.

While choosing colors that inspire you is essential to creating a room that makes you happy, artfully mixing different colors is equally important. A lot of elements—chairs, rugs, art, walls, accents, pillows—compete for attention in a room. Using too many colors or colors that don't harmonize will make a room feel unsettled.

helpful rules of thumb

1. Keep color under control. To create serene spaces, one helpful rule of thumb is to limit the number of colors in a room to three or four, with two of the colors in a palette serving as accents. Softer neutrals on walls result in more soothing rooms, introduce color with rugs, art and accents like pillows and lamps. Still, painting your walls is a great way to experiment with color. You can minimize your risk and your expense by painting a single wall a bolder, brighter or richer color. Similarly, you can paint the inside of a closet or bookshelf a stronger hue to work in color that can easily be changed with minimal expense and disruption if you tire of it or decide you don't like it.

2. Use strong color in small doses. Whether you're adding color with paint, fabric, accents or art, complex colors, such as brick red, slate blue, pear green, or ochre, are easier on the eye than bold hues or primary or secondary colors, which are better deployed in small doses (or in bright, sunny locations).

3. Limit contrast. Another helpful tip to create harmonious color schemes is to use colors that are adjacent to each other on the color wheel. They keep a room cohesive by minimizing contrast. You can mix lighter and darker shades of similar hues to keep things interesting. And be sure to sprinkle accents around the room, rather than group them in one place, to keep the eye moving and the scheme balanced.

4. Use shots of pattern. A final key to creating a pleasing palette is to use mostly solid blocks of color and limit pattern to smaller furnishings, accents or art. To create a soothing flow from room to room, keep the palette consistent throughout. You might switch the dominant hue from one room to the next for variety, but sticking to a unified palette in spaces that visually connect will keep them from feeling disjointed.

Expert Tips on Working with Color

• **Rely on a reference for cues.**
A vintage Oriental rug served as the starting point for all of the colors of the upholstery, cushions, and even the art in our living room. When choosing between the dominant and accent colors for the palette, I remembered a tip given to me by New York–based designer Jamie Drake, who suggested using the least prevalent color in the rug as the dominant color on the walls.

A curtain fabric, decorative bowl or work of art are also viable starting points for a color palette.
• **Consider the context.**
The geographical location of your home and the prevailing colors in the landscape or other buildings are also good starting points for color choices. In our apartment in India, for example, we've painted one wall in a bedroom a deep pink hue, which looks beautiful in the strong sun. In most parts of the U.S., on the other hand, super-bright colors look out of place.

• **Establish balance.**
When mixing colors, artists may use completely different hues, but the saturation or intensity of the colors is often similar.
• **Create a harmonious composition.** When using two colors in a palette, let one dominate by employing it through 70 to 80 percent of the scheme and use the other in 20 to 30 percent of the scheme.
• **Rely on cultural associations.** Use colors that resonate with cultural associations that are

meaningful to you, suggests Sonu Mathew, a color expert and spokeswoman for Benjamin Moore, who notes that most Americans respond positively to shades of red, white and blue. She also says that social media is creating a new platform for color associations. "You can now go to the top of Mount Kilamanjaro through the Internet without leaving your chair," she says. "This phenomenon is creating new communities with different color associations around the world."

Using Paint Color to Shape Spaces and Solve Problems

• **Make a room appear larger.** When painted on walls, pale shades of cool colors, such as sky blue, soft gray and misty lavender, look as though they recede and expand, like the sky, and so make rooms feel larger. By the same token, painting a ceiling white or pale blue will make a room feel taller.

• **Make a room feel cozier.** Walls painted with rich shades or warmer colors like red, taupe or cocoa brown will appear to advance and therefore make a room feel more intimate.

• **Create a focal point.** In a room devoid of character, using a strong color on a single wall will draw attention to a work of art or piece of furniture you want to highlight.

A word on wallpaper

Wallpaper has made a comeback recently—partly because fresh new patterns, colors and textures from a new crop of designers have elevated its appeal, but also because the challenge in removing it from walls has been resolved thanks to new advances in adhesive technology.

Available in many materials, from vinyl and grass cloth to eco-friendly materials made from recycled teabags and coffee filters, wallpaper is a great way to create a focal point by applying it to one wall. You can also use it to introduce an element of surprise, adhering it to the inside of a linen closet, for example, or to the back of a curio cabinets or set of bookshelves. Higher-quality papers made using a surface-printing technique developed in the 1830s, which allows the printing of up to 13 colors, look almost like fine art. One way to feature beautiful wallpapers like these is to frame them like murals without actually applying them to the wall.

For the pattern-phobic, textured wallpapers or a creamy-white one with a hint of iridescence can add dimension and durability to a hall or foyer—paint gets scuffed, but a highly engineered wallpaper can last for 30 years. New Easy-Up Easy-Down wallpapers make changing them very simple, and new developments in their construction allow seams to lock into place and require no booking (the laborious process of folding and soaking the wallpaper before applying), making the installation process easier than ever before. In addition, a new generation of artisans is offering wares directly to the consumer online, bypassing the traditional trade routes that made high-end papers accessible only through designers.

That said, installing wallpaper isn't a do-it-yourself job for most people. And given the range of costs for wallpaper from $25 to several hundred dollars a roll, if you want the pop of pattern and texture that wallpaper offers, it's best to contact a pro.

Wallpaper Source List

• **The National Guild of Professional Paperhangers:** A good starting point for research and assistance. *ngpp.org*.

• **Graham & Brown:** The UK wallpaper makers' pop-art prints are favored by decorators but are also available to consumers. *grahambrown.com*.

• **The Wallcoverings Association:** Another reliable source of information on a range of manufacturers. *wallcoverings.org*.

• **Anthropologie:** The boho-chic retailer has expanded its home decor offerings to include wallpapers from new designers like Timorous Beasties, Catherine Martin and Porridge and Patch. *anthropologie.com*.

• **DecoratorsBest:** An online showroom that offers consumers access to its wholesale inventory of wallpapers, along with helpful online calculators to help you redo your rooms. *decoratorsbest.com*.

• **York Wallcoverings:** The largest maker of wallcoverings in the U.S. offers a broad selection of wallpapers inspired by historic patterns as well as collections from

notable designers. *yorkwall.com*.

• **The Future Perfect:** New York's go-to destination for buzzed-about American and European talents, including Aimée Wilder, Osborne & Little, Trove and others. *thefutureperfect.com*.

• **Walnut Wallpaper:** This L.A.-based boutique offers upscale and vintage wallpapers to the trade and consumers. *walnutwallpaper.com*.

furniture and accents

Clarifying your sense of style doesn't have to mean sticking rigidly to a particular look. Introducing modern touches to traditional environments or an occasional antique to a contemporary setting will inject a room with energy, give it the flexibility to evolve over time, and keep it from looking dated. Mixing elements of different styles should be handled with care, however, to prevent your stylistic point of view from becoming diluted or devolving into an eclectic jumble.

While your furniture and accents are one part of the style equation, their placement is another. The impact of a beautiful antique or shapely side chair can be lost if it isn't positioned to best advantage and in harmony with the room and neighboring furnishings.

Comfortable and harmonious arrangements

Artfully arranging furniture is actually quite simple if you let the architecture of the room take the lead. Begin by noting points of entry, which will help you locate the primary and cross axis and enable you to identify the flow of traffic throughout the space. Then, depending on the size of the room, establish your seating group or groups around them.

To allow the shell of the room to read clearly as a volume, pull the furniture at least a few inches away from the wall, if possible, and allow it to float around a coffee table or ottoman. Intimate conversational areas take shape when the furniture is placed close to the table, rather than pushed out against the walls. At the same time, seating groups need enough breathing room—ideally at least 2½ to 3 feet between pieces—for easy circulation around the furnishings, through the room and into adjoining spaces. Seating groups that are contained and intimate are not only more comfortable, they're easier on the eye, too. By keeping the furnishings collected, the visual attention is focused, rather than scattered about the room. And the negative space around the furnishings allows the lines of each piece to register.

Other guides to furniture placement are the room's architectural focal points—a window overlooking a spectacular view, for example, or a fireplace. Place the furnishings so that the primary pieces permit unobstructed sightlines toward the focal point.

Scale and proportion

Recognizing the scale of a room—as well as the furnishings that will occupy it—will also help you to harmoniously shape the setting. Designers are masters at fooling the eye by playing with scale, using a tall curio cabinet or curtains mounted near the ceiling, for example, to exaggerate the scale of a small room, or deploying factions of furniture groups to bring a large room down to a more manageable size. But you still need to set off large elements with small ones to create a sense of balance. And ideally include midsize elements to bridge the gap and let the eye move easily from one scale to the next without uncomfortable visual leaps.

helpful rules of thumb

These ideas will help you arrange your furnishings and accents, and allow them to work together as harmonious ensembles.

1. **Clarify your point of view.** One way to successfully merge furnishings from different eras or of different styles is to follow the 20-80 rule of composition. If you want a fresh traditional ambience, for example, opt for a majority of traditional or traditionally inspired furnishings and brighten them with a small collection of modern pieces. The same holds true in reverse to create a softer modern environment.

2. **Define comfort zones.** One way to pull an intimate seating group together is to ground it with a rug. Just as scale and proportion establish harmony among individual pieces of furniture, a rug needs to complement the scale of a room and be large enough to link the separate pieces as an ensemble. At the very least, try to choose a rug that is large enough to fit the front legs of all the seating in your group.

3. **Highlight a focal point.** Whether it's an incredible view, a beautiful work of art, a stunning sofa or a simple fireplace, one aspect of your room should immediately grab your eye and allow it to focus before it travels around to the other furnishings and accents in a room. Ideally, this element will be on axis with the entrance to the room.

4. **Use color or materials to create unity.** Another way to link disparate furnishings is through color. You might cover most of your new and antique upholstered pieces in white fabric, for example. Or you might link wood pieces from different eras by choosing those made mostly with the same kind of wood or stained a similar color. Not everything needs to be linked in this way, but if most of your furnishings relate to one another through a common thread, they'll stand as a cohesive ensemble.

5. **Think in pairs.** The simplest way to create a sense of balance in a room is to introduce at least one pair of furnishings or accents. Place a pair of armchairs on either side of a sofa, top a mantel

with matching vases, or flank a door with matching sconces for an instant sense of balance and order.

6. **Use repetition.** Repeating elements throughout a room creates a sense of rhythm that brings a feeling of harmony to the ambience. Some ways to establish repetition include surrounding a series of botanical prints with matching frames, adding pops of pattern with throw pillows covered in the same fabric, or suspending three pendant fixtures in a row over a countertop.

7. **Introduce contrast.** As in a work of art, contrast brings a sense of harmony to a space and allows the eye to move about the room and discern shapes and silhouettes. There are many ways to add contrast. You can set off something heavy, like a sofa, with something light, like a skeletal coffee table with slender legs. You can also play off dark elements, like wooden chairs or tables, against a creamy background.

8. **Mix geometric shapes.** One way to ensure that a room retains its energy is to include pieces with different shapes. Play circular pieces, which bring a sense of movement and energy to a room, off square or rectangular ones, which introduce a grounding, stabilizing quality. You can also position different pieces to create implied shapes. By topping an entry console with a round mirror, you'll create the suggestion of a triangular shape, as the eye fills in the lines that extend from the edges of the horizontal plane of the console up to the top of the mirror.

9. **Pay attention to scale and proportion.** In general, smaller scale furnishings work better in small rooms and larger-scale pieces are better suited to large ones—but a carefully edited mix of both will lend more interest to the room.

soft furnishings

No room is complete without soft furnishings—sleek draperies, graceful window shades, pretty cushions, cozy throws, luscious bed linens. Not only do fabric elements add beauty, color, warmth, softness and personality to a room, they're incredibly practical, too.

Think of soft furnishings as the grace notes that balance the hard surfaces and angles in a room and address the finer points of comfort. Curtains can bring in softness and color while providing privacy and controlling harsh sunlight, for example. A slipcover, on the other hand, can transition a more formal upholstered chair from winter to spring while extending the life of the upholstery and protecting it from stains at the same time. And, as seasons and styles change, soft furnishings, such as pillows, throws, napkins and table linens, are among the easiest pieces to switch out to freshen up a room cost-effectively.

defining goals

Given the countless colors, patterns and textures of decorative fabrics from which soft furnishings are made—as well as the endless ways in which fabrics can be shaped into wonderful forms—it helps to return to your stylistic frame of reference to guide your choices in both the fabrics and the style of your soft furnishings themselves. If you're developing a traditional-style setting, for example, you might choose floor-length draperies topped with a pleated valance to frame a window. If a modern scheme is what you're after, then you might opt for crisp Roman shades.

Once you hone in on the look you're after, consider the functional goals for your soft furnishings, too, as well as what you're willing to spend to create them. Custom curtains can cost a bundle, but they can also last 25 years or more, meaning you'll amortize their cost over time if you plan to stay in your home for the long haul. Decorative pillows on the other hand can be purchased for next to nothing, and can readily be replaced for an instant style update while keeping your budget in check.

tips on using fabric effectively

Before investing in soft furnishings for your home, consider these tips for making stylish and savvy choices.

* **Keep upholstered pieces simple.** Especially in public rooms, the fabrics on large upholstered items should be easy on the eye, and preferably in a solid color. It's easier to switch out a printed pillow when you tire of it than to start over with a new chair fabric. Solid blocks of color on furnishings will also make a room feel more serene, and will provide a solid base that you can change simply with accents, pillows, rugs and art.

* **Consider your lifestyle.** If you've got a large family, young children or pets, know that your upholstered pieces will endure a fair share of wear and tear, so be sure the fabric you choose is durable and dirt-resistant, too. Opt for textured fabrics such as tweeds or chenilles, or look for a high-performance fabric, such as a synthetic ultra-suede, that's durable and stain-resistant, too. If you're a low-maintenance empty nester, you might go for silk or velvet.

✳ **Expand your options.** If you want a seasonal change of scene, consider slipcovers. They can be made in different colors and fabrics to give a chair a completely different look during different times of year. Slipcovers can also extend the upholstery life of new sofas and chairs by protecting them from the fading rays of the sun as well as dirt and grime.

✳ **Use pattern sparingly.** Even if you love pattern, limiting it to smaller doses will help keep a room feeling serene. Employ it on small side chairs, pillows or ottomans for best effect. Patterned rugs are also great, as they conceal footprints and dirt.

✳ **Choose curtain fabric with care.** Curtains bring softness and drama to bare windows, but patterns sometimes lose their impact when lost in folds of fabric, so prefer solids and neutrals for curtains and shades. If you do choose a patterned fabric for a window treatment, however, consider the scale of the pattern in relation to the scale of the windows and other patterned elements in the room.

✳ **Be mindful of curtain headers and hems.** If, for example, you're creating custom curtains in a traditional home, you might choose softer goblet pleats, butterfly pleats or fan pleats; for a modern home you might opt for clean panels topped with crisp pinch pleats, X pleats or grommets. For very soft romantic headers, a variety of header tapes can be employed to create gathered, shirred or smocked designs. For more casual rooms, consider panels topped with tabs, ties or clip-on rings. Pocket-style headers always result in soft or romantic curtains.

Another key to stylish curtains is their length. Ideally, they should break at the floor an inch or two, like well-made gentleman's trousers, for an elegant drape. However, many people prefer curtains that stop just short of the floor for ease of cleaning, which is also fine. Short curtains should be hemmed just above the windowsill.

✳ **Vary the scale of patterns.** Including fabrics in a mix of large-, medium- and small-scale patterns will also keep the overall picture balanced. Also, remember that the style and scale of the pattern should relate not only to the style of the piece of furniture but also to its size and proportions.

✳ **Add a personal touch.** Give extra polish to pillows you make yourself or inject a ready-made pillow with a custom touch by embellishing a pillow cover with trims and embellishments. Piping or welting provides a classic finish to the seams of all kinds of cushions, from a basic toss pillow to an extravagant neck roll. Other options for edging cushions are narrow flanges and brush fringe.

✳ **Choose fabrics in soothing hues for bedrooms.** Fabrics with limited patterns and soft hands will also contribute a serene and comforting ambience.

shaping comfortable spaces with light

Even though light itself is immaterial, it profoundly affects our experience of space. While the light fixtures are important parts of the material style mix, the quality of the light they generate affects not only how a room functions, but more important, how it feels. It has the power to make or break a mood.

Lighting designers regard light as a medium, like an artist views paint, and they use it to shape our perception of space by highlighting architectural elements, creating focal points, subtly washing walls with gradations of illumination, or creating contrast with brightness and shadows. Richard Kelly, a celebrated 20th-century lighting designer who is widely recognized as one of the founders of the modern architectural lighting profession, produced the lighting schemes for houses and buildings created by some of the most highly regarded architects of the 20th century, including Philip Johnson, Mies van der Rohe and Louis Kahn, among others. He used light to influence a person's experience of architecture—its forms, materials, scale, proportion, color, decoration, even its sense of durability and stability. He also defined three elemental kinds of light effects that can be used to influence the perception of any space, and these definitions of light continue to guide lighting designers today. He described these qualities of light as focal glow, ambient luminescence, and the play of brilliants—and anyone can work with these qualities to create visually appealing illumination.

Focal glow: To clarify these qualities of light, Kelly compared each to the ways we commonly experience light. "Focal glow is the 'follow spot' on the modern stage, it is the pool of light on your favorite reading chair, the shaft of sunlight that warms the far end of the valley, candlelight on a face or a flashlight's beam," he said. "Focal glow draws attention, pulls together diverse parts, sells merchandise, separates the important from the unimportant, helps people see." The types of fixtures that create focal glow are reading and floor lamps or pendant fixtures with shades that control and direct the light in a very focused way.

Ambient luminescence: In contrast, according to Kelly, this second type of light is diffuse and unfocused. "Ambient luminescence is the uninterrupted light of a snowy morning in the open country, fog light at sea in a small boat, twilight haze on a river where shore and water and sky are indistinguishable," he said. Instead of focusing light on a single area and giving importance to a certain object or feature by highlighting it, this type of light produces shadowless illumination. In other words, it is indirect lighting that minimizes form, in effect equalizing the importance of objects and people. It is usually reassuring, quiets the nerves and is restful. This type of light is generally produced by fixtures that cast light upward, bouncing it off the ceiling so that it indirectly illuminates a space. It is also often created with overhead fixtures that are covered with frosted shades that diffuse the light. Daylight entering a space through sheers or scrim shades is also a form of ambient illumination.

The play of brilliants: In identifying the third quality of light, Kelly used a term commonly used in the jewelry business. According to Kelly, "The play of brilliants is Times Square at night, an 18th-century ballroom with a crystal chandelier of many candle lamps. It is sunlight on a fountain or brook, a cache of diamonds in an open cave, the rose window at Chartres cathedral, night automobiles at a busy cloverleaf, a city at night from the air, the trees outside your window interlaced with the beams of a spotlight or a shaft of sunlight, a sparkling cabinet of glassware." Unlike the soothing effect of ambient illumination or highlighting quality of focused light, this type of light "excites the optic nerve and in turn stimulates the body and spirit, quickens the appetite, awakens curiosity, sharpens the wit," said Kelly. Also commonly referred to as "sparkle," this type of light is produced by fixtures such as crystal sconces, candles, Christmas lights and even shiny reflective elements, such as pieced mirrors, silverware or other metal surfaces that refract light and make it flicker or twinkle.

Ultimately, designers understand that the beauty of designed spaces, indoors or out, is best perceived when all three of these kinds of light are at play, though one usually dominates. Focal glow makes it easier to see, ambient illumination makes surroundings feel safe and reassuring, and the play of brilliants stimulates the spirit. Keeping these ideas in mind when designing a room, or a landscape, will allow you to artfully shape the space with light.

tips on placing light fixtures

Light fixtures are among the most sculptural and decorative elements you can add to your home. It's important to choose pieces

✱ Move outlets off the wall. Install outlets in the floor if your furniture floats in the center of the room, to keep unsightly cords contained and prevent them from tripping someone.

✱ Ensure clear vision. Try to keep the bottom of the lampshade of a floor lamp at about eye level of a seated person to prevent glare.

✱ Position sconces for easy passage. If you illuminate a hall with sconces, mount them about 6 to 8 feet apart for even illumination and about 5 feet from the floor to keep light around eye level.

Tip: Use frosted bulbs to soften the glow of a chandelier in a dining room to diminish shadows on faces.

art and collectibles

While the furnishings in a room establish its style, art has the potential to express its soul. A colorful abstract piece can animate a serene room, a portrait can lend an air of formality, an atmospheric landscape can soothe. Given art's transformative power, the placement of the art and its frame need to support its role as a visual and emotional focal point. Still, art, like furniture, is part of a larger context. When choosing and placing art for our own home, I have found a simple idea from the designer Mariette Himes Gomez to be a valuable guide: "Art follows furniture, not furniture art."

If you want your art to be a coherent part of your environs, select pieces that click with your point of view. You might choose pieces that contrast with your furniture—abstract works in traditional rooms, for example. Or you might choose pieces from a particular genre or period.

Art doesn't have to be costly to have value. When framed and presented as a group, even a series of children's drawings can make a lively impact in a room. A collection of vintage posters can be a graphic statement. Botanical prints at purchased at flea markets or photographs with similar subjects, such as trees, doors or stones, are other affordable alternatives, especially if you frame or shoot them yourself.

Collections of objects, such as wooden boxes, ceramic pots, wooden cutting boards, wire birdcages or butter molds—when carefully edited—can also be assembled into groups and presented like a work of art to transform a dead wall into a focal point. For example, designer Ingrid Leess mounted shelves across the width of a wall to display her collection of ceramic vases (see page 158). Consisting of mostly white pieces with clean lines, the collection is easy to take in as a whole. Designer Nestor Santa-Cruz, on the other hand, likes to identify a client's favorite object and make it the most important piece in the room.

that not only complement your decor, but are proportionate with the architecture and furnishings. The following tips will help you select and position them most effectively:

✱ Balance scales. Even if lamps flanking a bed or sofa don't match, choose fixtures that have similar visual weight.

✱ Be mindful of size. When suspending pendants or chandeliers over a table or kitchen island, be sure they are at least 9 or 10 inches smaller in diameter or width than the table or island so that no one bumps while leaning forward.

✱ Gauge the distance. If you have an 8-foot-high ceiling, suspend a pendant or chandelier so that the bottom of the fixture is positioned approximately 30 inches above the tabletop. Increase the height of the fixture 3 inches for every additional foot of ceiling height. Chandeliers and pendants also allow you to highlight the vertical access or center of a room.

When well placed or highlighted, he says, this object will always bring a smile to owner. What's important is that collectibles resonate not only with your furnishings, but also with the other art and objects in a room or adjoining rooms.

tips on displaying art

✳ **Photographs gain stature and cohesion** when surrounded with matching frames and hung as a collection.

✳ **Edit your collections** with a judicious eye, eliminating all but the pieces you really love. Rotating new pieces in and old ones out will allow your objects to continue to stimulate you and be free of clichés.

✳ **Art and accessories needn't come from the same era** or be of similar style to work together, but they do need a common thread, such as a color, material or an idea. In this way, the objects will capture attention and tell a story about the collector.

✳ **A painting or print looks best when mounted** so that the center of the piece is at eye level for an average-height person—about 66 inches from the floor. If you have several works of art mounted in this way, they'll be linked by an invisible horizon line that will bring a sense of balance to the room.

✳ **Give small works stature** by surrounding them with large mats. Or mount them in proportionate frames in a group where they can be viewed from close proximity.

✳ **Place a small painting on an easel** on a table with other objects, or lean a midsize piece against the wall atop a mantel.

✳ **Consult a lighting professional** about placement if you want to use recessed lighting to highlight art. Some fixtures need to be placed 30 inches away from the art and spaced 24 inches apart to evenly wash the painting with light and prevent the scallops that appear from the spread of the light beams. But lighting technology continues to evolve, so a standard like this is subject to change. Usually, the lighting you use to illuminate the room is sufficient to highlight the art, so you don't necessarily need special lighting unless you want to call attention to the art. Just be sure to keep high-quality art out of the direct line of the sun.

◉ *Art and Framing Resources*
ArtWeLove.com, LarsonJuhl.com, Chelsea Frames, Art.com

A Word on Order

Casually tossed pillows and throws, a small stack of books on a table, and a motley mix of framed photos on a shelf can give a room a lived-in feeling that actually enhances a decorating scheme. But even a little bit of clutter can instantly disrupt the visual harmony of a room. The following tips will help you integrate storage and corral clutter so that the odds and ends of daily life can become part of the decor rather than detract from it.

• **Put your best face forward.** Carefully edit the objects you put on open shelves—even in the kitchen. Utilitarian objects like drinking glasses or utensils are easy on the eye when they're all of a single material, such as wood, glass or stainless steel, or all of a single color. The same holds true for more decorative objects, like vases, covered boxes or picture frames displayed on open bookshelves or in the cubbies of a television armoire.

• **Create symmetry.** Instead of placing a lone bookshelf along a wall, make a pair of freestanding bookshelves look like part of the architecture by using them to flank a fireplace or door and wrapping them with crown and baseboard molding.

• **Use containers.** Baskets, woven boxes and even garden urns add texture and form while providing a spot to stow little stuff, like remote controls, cell phones, newspapers and magazines.

• **Incorporate double-duty furnishings.** Furniture manufacturers are now offering more furnishings with integrated storage than ever before. Ottomans double as storage cubes, while desk armoires contain slide-out panels and overhead shelves that can be hidden from view with the close of a door when not in use. Built-in features, like pullout drawers in window seats or doors in television armoires, put items out of sight at the end of the day or during a party.

• **Cover up.** Crisp fabric toppers over side or hall tables or skirts around pedestal sinks can hide all kinds of odds and ends—from rubber boots and umbrellas to hairbrushes and razor blades.

sustainability

these days, most everyone wants a greener home. But sorting through the subtleties of sustainable building materials, furnishings and practices can be overwhelming. Going green may involve making trade-offs, as there are many ways to measure and practice eco-friendly design, which confounds decision-making even more. Yet demand for green design continues to grow, so eco-friendly manufacturing and building standards and practices are continuously being codified by industry leaders and third-party certifiers.

And this means some aspect of eco-friendliness is becoming standard in many of the home furnishings and products produced today, making green living easier than ever before.

When shopping for products for your home—from paint and wallpaper to flooring and furniture—it's helpful to have a sense of the benchmarks by which green design is currently evaluated, so that you can make informed decisions. Having resources on hand that can help you make choices based on your values, vision, goals and budget is also a plus. Federal, state and local incentives, rebates and tax breaks make going green more affordable now, too. The pages that follow will provide you with the information you need to make your home as eco-friendly and healthy as it can be.

what is a green home?

In many ways, houses are like people. They have a protective exterior skin, a skeletal structure, and internal systems that require fuel and maintenance to function properly. And the greener a house is, the healthier it will be for its occupants and the planet. Whether your home is old or new, if your goal is to make it greener, then it's worth knowing the current minimum green building standards established by the primary national, regional and local government agencies and

green home certification programs in this country, all of which aim to accomplish the same essential goals. In general, the guidelines of these agencies and organizations aspire to make homes greener by doing the following:

- Minimizing environmental impact by wasting fewer resources during site preparation, construction or renovation
- Recycling and conserving water and materials
- Reducing carbon buildup
- Using sustainable and nontoxic materials and finishes whenever possible
- Ensuring good indoor air quality
- Creating structures that are at least 15 percent more energy-efficient than those built with standard construction practices

Among the most well-known providers of green building standards are the U.S. Environmental Protection Agency and the U.S. Department of Energy, whose joint Energy Star and Water Sense programs aim to help consumers save money and protect the environment through energy-efficient products and conservation practices. Two other national nonprofit organizations, the National Association of Home Builders and the U.S. Green Building Council, also offer guidelines and certification programs for green design. The LEED criteria and guidelines developed by the USGBC are generally considered the gold standard by which environmental design is judged. (LEED stands for Leadership in Energy and Environmental Design.)

why be eco-friendly?

There are many benefits to living in a green home. In general, though, it will have a positive influence on three primary aspects of your life.

Your health: Foremost among the benefits of greening your home is that it's good for your health. Green homes rely on natural ventilation as well as mechanical ventilation systems that filter and bring fresh air in and vent stale air out to keep indoor air clean. Good green homes also use toxin-free materials and finishes or those with low toxicity to limit indoor air pollution, which can be more harmful than pollution outdoors. Green homes are also designed to maximize natural light, which not only boosts your mood, but is also vital to indoor plants, which are natural air detoxifiers. And some green materials and home products resist mold and mildew or are antimicrobial, making for an all-around healthier indoor environment.

Green Guidelines

For more information on various national, regional and local green building organizations and programs, visit these sites:
- *energystar.gov:* For information on the federal government's Energy Star and WaterSense programs
- *nahb.org:* For the National Association of Home Builders' green building guidelines and certification for its members
- *usgbc.org:* For the U.S. Green Building Council's Leadership in Energy and Environmental Design (LEED) program's green residential certification standards
- *healthhouse.org:* For guidelines recommended by Health House,

a program of the American Lung Association that aims to encourage home construction that meets the most stringent building standards in the U.S. and includes site inspections during construction and performance testing upon completion
- *greenhomeguide.com:* For information on guidelines for green practices for renovation and remodeling of existing homes developed by the American Society of Interior Designers in partnership with the U.S. Green Building Council. The site also offers information on more than 70 other regional and local green building home programs throughout the U.S.

Your bank account: Living in a green house is also good for your pocketbook. Tax incentives or rebates and energy savings can make building a new green home or greening an existing home more cost-effective than building and living in a standard house. On a month-to-month basis, people who live in green homes save money by consuming less energy and less water than those who live in standard homes, which reduces their energy and utility bills. Green homes are also often more durable than most standard homes, thanks to high-quality building materials and construction processes, which lead to lower maintenance costs and fewer repairs. Furthermore, the value of a green home is often higher than that of a comparable standard home, particularly because the market demand for green homes is on the rise.

Local, state and federal governments as well as utility companies have been offering tax breaks and other incentives for building certified green homes or adding green features to your home, as long as they meet accepted green guidelines. In the near future, green homes will likely cost less to insure than standard homes, too.

What Is a Net Zero Energy Home?

A Net Zero Energy Home combines state-of-the-art, energy-efficient construction and appliances with commercially available renewable energy systems, such as solar water heating and solar electricity. The combination results in a home that produces its own energy— as much or more than it needs. Even though the home might be connected to a utility grid, it has net zero energy consumption from the utility provider. A Net Zero Energy Home can be designed to continue functioning even during blackouts, and the fact that such a home produces energy protects its owner from fluctuations in energy prices.

Opposite: Painted white, a recycled brass chandelier brightens the dining area of a recently renovated home. New windows improve views and energy efficiency. Right: A new deck made of durable western red cedar allows the owners to take advantage of ocean views outdoors.

Your planet: Green homes are also easy on the environment and often use up to 40 percent less energy than similar standard homes. If you use drought-tolerant landscaping, efficient plumbing and bathing fixtures, and water-conservation systems, your home will also use less water than standard homes. Many green building materials are made with recycled content, which also minimizes impact on the environment. Salvaged materials from demolished buildings are also often used in green homes, as are materials made from rapidly renewable materials, such as bamboo, hemp and soybean-based products. In addition, the use of specially certified woods helps promote socially and environmentally beneficial forestry practices.

eco-friendly remodeling and upgrades

Whether you're planning to undertake a major remodeling effort or simply make some minor upgrades, virtually every element in the home can be made more eco-friendly. The pages that follow offer a summary of all the major indoor residential building components and green improvements you can make.

windows and doors

Windows and doors help define the character of your home, but advancements in how they're made mean they now play a significant role in improving energy efficiency, too. Most window and door manufacturers offer tools on their websites that can help you select new or replacement windows and doors that suit your energy, aesthetic and budgetary requirements. Look for these energy-saving characteristics.

Energy efficiency and UV protection: To increase energy efficiency and comfort in your home, choose Energy Star–rated dual pane, low-e windows. And in very cold climates, ask for windows with three or more panes. These qualities should also be sought in exterior doors with decorative windows or sidelights. If your budget doesn't allow for the purchase of new windows, you can apply UV window film to your windows that can help improve their effectiveness and efficiency. Various window films from 3M, for example, not only reduce the effects of solar heat and visible light on your furnishings, but will block 99 percent of the sun's harmful ultraviolet rays and provide up to a 79 percent reduction in the sun's heat, reducing the cost of your energy bill.

Resources for Green Incentives

For more information on the many local and state governments, utility companies and other entities that offer rebates, tax breaks and other incentives that may be available in your area, visit these websites:

• *energy.gov/taxbreaks.htm:* As a result of the Energy Policy Act of 2005, the U.S. government offers various tax breaks and incentives for energy-efficient upgrades to homes.
• *dsireusa.org:* The Database of State Incentives for Renewables & Efficiency is a nonprofit project funded by the U.S. Department of Energy through the North Carolina Solar Center and the Interstate Renewable Energy Council. It provides information on local, state, federal and utility incentives available for switching to renewable or efficient energy use.
• *epa.gov/greenbuilding/tools/funding.htm:* The U.S. Environmental Protection Agency's site offers information on sources of incentives for green building available at the national, state and local levels for homeowners.
• *energystar.gov/index.cfm?c=tax_credits.tx_index:* The U.S. government's site for its Energy Star program provides insight on how consumers, home builders and others can get federal tax credits for using energy-efficient products.

Right: Painted with low-VOC paint, wall paneling and cabinets made from wood certified by the Forest Stewardship Council is an eco-friendly choice. Opposite: Wallpapers from York, including the Flourish pattern shown here, are made with efficient printing processes to reduce environmental impact.

Weatherstripping: Doors with new frames may also include a magnetic strip to create a tighter seal that reduces air and water leakage and noise and makes your home more energy-efficient. Many types of weatherstripping are made from synthetic materials, such as neoprene, polypropylene nylon or urethane foam. Brass and stainless steel weatherstripping, available at many hardware stores, can be a less toxic alternative.

paneling, paints, stains and wallpaper

Paneling, molding, millwork and trim: For eco-friendly wall paneling, molding and other architectural elements, such as beadboard, board-and-batten, wainscoting, crown molding, and other trims made of wood or wood byproducts, choose products certified by a recognized third-party verifier, such as the Forest Stewardship Council or the Sustainable Forestry Initiative, if you can. When marked with their seals, products made with wood or wood byproducts are certified to come from responsibly managed forests. Another green option is to use reclaimed lumber products salvaged from other architectural locations.

Paints: Paint is the most common finish used on interior walls, but it can also perpetrate indoor air pollution. While the range in toxicity and performance characteristics of latex paints is vast, numerous low- or no-VOC paints have recently become widely available. Federal regulations set the VOC content limit in paint at 250 grams per liter. To easily identify low- or no-VOC paints, look for products that feature a Green Seal, the mark of approval by an independent group of the same name that sets standards for eco-conscious goods.

Wallpapers: If you want to use a wallcovering in a sustainable way, search for one made with natural materials that can be applied with low-toxicity adhesive. Or use a brand that relies on eco-friendly printing and manufacturing practices, such as many of the brands produced by York, the largest wallpaper manufacturer in America, which has a new line of contract wallpapers from Candice Olson, among other products, that are low-VOC. Other sources of eco-friendly wallpapers include Adrienne Neff, which uses low-VOC water-based inks on stock made of post-consumer polycellulose fiber paper, and The Wallpaper Collective, which offers paper by the eco-conscious designer Beware the Moon, which prints on FSC-certified papers using water-based inks. Both offer their wares directly to the consumer online. Visit *adrienneneff.com* or *wallpapercollective.com*.

Eco-Friendly Resource

Green Seal is an independent nonprofit organization that strives to achieve a healthier environment by identifying and certifying green products and services. Windows and doors that are Green Seal–certified meet the organization's energy-efficiency requirements and are manufactured and packaged in a consistent, environmentally responsible manner. Visit *greenseal.org*.

What are VOCs?

If being in a freshly painted room gives you a sore throat, itchy eyes or a headache, you may be reacting to the volatile organic compounds (VOCs) in the solvents added to many paints. As the paint dries, the VOCs release gases. Exposure to these gases can be especially difficult for environmentally sensitive people or asthma sufferers, and long-term exposure can cause health problems. VOCs may include carcinogenic chemicals such as acetone, toluene, xylene, formaldehyde and benzenes, and they also outgas from stains, adhesives and synthetic flooring.

cabinets and counters

cabinets

Cabinets can eat up roughly half of the average budget for a kitchen remodel, according to the National Kitchen & Bath Association, a trade group that trains and certifies kitchen designers. And cabinets are often composed of materials that contain urea formaldehyde, which contributes to indoor air pollution and causes a wide range of adverse health effects, including headaches, skin rashes, burning and itchy eyes, sore nose and throat, nausea and possibly even cancer, according to the U.S. EPA.

Cabinet doors are often made with solid wood or wood veneers, but because wood expands and contracts with changes in air temperature and humidity, cabinet boxes or shells are typically made, for dimensional stability, of interior-grade plywood or pressed wood products, such as particleboard or MDF, most of which are made with formaldehyde as a binder. Although manufacturers have reduced emissions in pressed wood products by 80 to 90 percent over the past 25 years or so and emissions drop off considerably a few months after installation, some products can continue to outgas for years. Furthermore, cabinets can be treated with harmful solvent-based stains and finishes, which also contribute to degrading indoor air quality.

◉ Eco-Wise Wood Cabinet Certifiers
For more information on green-certified woods, visit these sites:
- *Forest Stewardship Council: info.fsc.org*
- *Sustainable Forestry Initiative: sfiprogram.org*
- *The Kitchen Cabinet Manufacturers Association: greencabinetsource.org*

consider the following eco-friendly options

- **Recycle or revamp existing cabinets.** The eco-friendliest choice you can make is to continue using your existing cabinets. If you've got wood cabinets with a worn finish, you can give them a lift by refinishing them with a low- or no-VOC paint. If you're handy you can do this yourself. Cabinet repair companies can also reface wood veneer or laminate cabinets. If the layout of your kitchen works for you, you can also upgrade cabinets by replacing just the doors.

- **Choose sustainably forested wood or wood-byproduct cabinets.** According to the National Kitchen & Bath Association, wood is the number one choice for cabinets in this country. If you opt for cabinets made from wood or wood veneers, choose those made with woods certified by the Forest Stewardship Council or the Sustainable Forestry Initiative, which are respected third-party organizations that evaluate wood products manufacturers for their forestry and environmentally safe manufacturing practices. Also look for cabinets made from FSC-certified particleboard or Medite II, a formaldehyde-free recycled wood fiber product, rather than conventional MDF.

- **Consider eco-friendly wood alternatives.** Some cabinets are now made with a product called wheatboard, which is a compressed straw fiber product made without formaldehyde binders.

- **Avoid exotic woods.** Do not choose cabinets made from tropical or exotic hardwoods, especially zebrawood and ebony, unless they are FSC-certified. A lack of control in overseas forests and the high-embodied energy involved in transporting these products do not make them wise green choices.

counters

From a green point of view, a good counter surface is nonporous, stain- and scratch-resistant, locally produced, nontoxic and beautiful. None of the counter surface materials currently available in the market meet all of these criteria, however. The countertop comparison that follows can help you sort through the pros and cons.

- **Stone:** Stones, such as marble, granite, slate and soapstone are beautiful, durable, heatproof and waterproof. Slate is nonporous and nonstaining. Granite comes in a variety of beautiful colors and patterns and is very hard, making it extremely stain- and scratch-resistant. It also holds up to heat and looks substantial. It is expensive, however, and requires periodic sealing with an impregnating finish. The mining of any stone has a negative impact on the envi-

Healthy Surface Help

Inexpensive testing kits for radon in granite and other stone counters are available at hardware stores or online sources. If you use one of these kits and it shows elevated levels from your home's surfaces, you should have an independent certified testing lab conduct another test to pinpoint the source. For more info, go to *epa.gov*/radon or call the National Radon Hotline at 800-SOS-RADON.

Another source for information on various environmentally friendly surfaces and other household products is the Greenguard Environmental Institute (GEI). Visit the organization's site at *greenguard.org*.

ronment, as all are finite resources. Stone should be tested for radon or radioactivity before installation. Look for a local source to reduce energy expended in transportation, seek out remnant slabs and finish with a low-VOC sealant.

• **Engineered stone:** Composed of quartz particles and resin, it is available in a larger range of colors than granite and has a nonporous surface that resists scratches, stains and heat. It's hygienic, easy to maintain and does not require sealing. It is heavy and expensive, and requires professional installation. The mining of the quartz impacts the environment, but it is safe and hygienic.

• **Solid surfaces:** Made by such companies as Avonite, Corian and Swanstone, nonporous solid-surface countertops are custom-made to your specifications and come in a rainbow of colors and patterns. They're made from synthetic acrylics or polyesters, so they're durable, seamless and stain-resistant, and scratches can be sanded out. These surfaces can be damaged by hot pans, however. They can range from moderately expensive to more expensive than granite or marble.

• **Ceramic tile:** Ceramic tile is often inexpensive, durable and easy to clean. It is also heatproof and stain- and water-resistant, and comes in a wide range of prices, colors, textures and designs. Tiles can easily chip or crack and grout lines can stain. Be sure to use non-toxic grouts and adhesives. Tile is generally inert and biodegradable.

• **Laminates:** Made of paper raw materials, laminates are low-cost and have smooth surfaces that are easy to clean. They are also available in a wide range of colors. Brands include Formica, Nevamar and Wilsonart. Scratches and chips are almost impossible to repair, though, and their seams show. They are also finished with petrochemical-based resin. Adhesives used to adhere the product to a particleboard surface can be toxic. Particleboard, interior-grade plywood and MDF substrates can outgas formaldehyde, unless FSC-certified. If you choose a laminate, get one that is Greenguard-certified.

• **Wood or butcher block:** Wood countertops are warm and beautiful and come in a wide range of colors, finishes and prices. They are easy to clean and can be sanded and resealed as needed, but their porous surface can harbor mold growth and stains easily. Wood can also be damaged by water and heat. Scratches must be oiled or sealed according to the manufacturer's instructions. Wood is a renewable resource. Finish wood counters with an odorless, nontoxic oil, such as walnut oil.

• **Stainless steel:** This nonporous, nonstaining surface is easy to clean and offers a sleek, industrial look for contemporary kitchens. It is also heat-resistant and durable. But it is expensive, noisy and may dent. You can't cut foods on a steel surface, and it conducts electricity, so proper ground fault interrupters are required to prevent possible electrocution. Mining for materials and the fabrication process required to make steel uses a large amount of energy and pollutes the environment. But it is often made of recycled content and can be recycled.

• **Composite and recycled materials:** Composite and recycled materials offer interesting aesthetic alternatives. Some are made from recycled paper and combined with resins to form a hard surface that is warmer than stone, and others are made from recycled glass, granite or other aggregates and are held together with either cement or resin to make a terrazzo-like surface. Durability and stain resistance varies depending on the product. Look for low-VOC resin usage, and in the case of paper products, look for FSC certification.

flooring

According to the World Floor Covering Association, green flooring includes any surface that is sustainable, recyclable or contains recycled content, leaves a small carbon footprint or has low levels of VOCs. Apart from the walls and ceilings, floors account for the largest surface area in your home, so they'll have a major impact on indoor air quality. The following summary highlights some primary characteristics of common floor materials.

• **Bamboo:** While many people think of bamboo as a wood, it is actually the world's largest growing grass. Though widely regarded as an eco-friendly choice because of its ability to quickly regenerate, no bamboo is currently certified as meeting various environmental production or preservation standards. Bamboo flooring is hard, more so than many hardwoods, and can last from 30 to 50 years. It will also biodegrade in landfills after it is removed, or it can be burned for energy. It ranges between $4 and $8 per square foot.

• **Stone:** Stone is a nonrenewable natural product that's durable and easy to maintain. According to the World Floor Covering Association, there is no generally accepted data on the environmental impact of using stone as flooring. But it is recyclable and can be reclaimed, and is quarried and manufactured using best practices. Stone is minimally processed, but quarrying, cutting, polishing and transporting this heavy material requires a lot of energy. Quarrying also impacts the

Eco-Friendly Carpet Labeling

The Green Label and Green Label Plus programs from the Carpet and Rug Institute also provide customers with the means by which to know whether they are purchasing the lowest VOC-emitting carpet, adhesive and cushion products available on the market. To achieve the Carpet and Rug Institute's Green Label Plus certification, a carpet must meet California's most rigorous 01350 standard, which tests for emissions of individual VOCs rather than just the overall level of VOCs.

• **Hardwood:** Hardwood is a wonderful green floor choice because it is natural, renewable, durable and recyclable. To be sure your hardwood is as green as possible, choose either reclaimed or salvaged wood floors from another site, or be sure new wood flooring is certified as environmentally friendly by an accredited certifier. Some hardwood flooring is engineered, meaning that instead of solid hardwood, it is made of several layers of wood material with a hardwood veneer. If you choose an engineered wood, opt for a certified floor, as the substrates of engineered wood floors are often made of wood byproducts bonded with substances that can contain toxic elements. Wood itself outgases minimally and does not harbor dust mites or mold. But wood floors require sealing, so choose sealers that give off few or no VOCs. Engineered and solid wood floors usually range from $3 to $6 per square foot.

• **Laminate:** Laminate flooring is a versatile, durable, attractive flooring with the appearance of a hardwood, tile or stone floor. Laminate floors are made up of several layers of materials, often including a moisture-resistant layer under a layer of HDF (high-density fiberboard) and topped with a high-resolution photographic image of natural wood flooring. Makers of laminate flooring argue that it is environmentally friendly as it uses less wood in its construction than solid wood or engineered wood floors and it makes more efficient use of the wood fiber, sawdust or wood chips that are used as its substrate. But it may also contain formaldehyde or other toxic substances. Look for a FloorScore seal on laminate flooring or check its VOC emissions, which confirms it meets today's most stringent emissions standards. It starts at about $2.50 per square foot.

• **Linoleum:** In use since the mid-1800s, linoleum has many environmental benefits that are fueling its comeback. The natural raw materials used to create linoleum—linseed oil, pine resin, wood flour, cork flour, ecologically responsible pigments and jute—are available in abundance. It does not release harmful substances or gases, and its patterns are dyed all the way through to the backing, ensuring even

surrounding landscape and water tables. Stone flooring can endure for centuries and can be disposed of safely or crushed and reused as aggregate for other building materials. Its price generally ranges from $3 to $10 per square foot.

• **Cork:** Cork is a unique renewable resource in that only the bark is harvested without damaging or destroying the tree. According to the WFCA, cork floors are made from the waste of cork used to make wine stoppers. If possible, choose all-natural cork flooring over cork-vinyl composites that have PVC backing. Cork flooring preserves its shape well and naturally resists mold and moisture. It's also durable, biodegradable and nontoxic. It costs about $3 to $6 per square foot.

• **Ceramic and glass tile:** Used as flooring for thousands of years, ceramic tile is durable, rarely releases emissions, requires little maintenance, and can contain recycled content from lightbulbs, ground glass and other materials. It is also made from abundant natural clays. But its weight demands the use of more fuel for transportation than other products. If tiles are glazed, they are highly moisture- and stain-resistant. If unglazed, they are more porous and not as smooth to the touch. Ceramic tile biodegrades after removal. Tiles can be reused and may also be crushed and recycled as aggregate materials. Generally, it costs between $1 to $6 per square foot.

wear; it's also biodegradable. Linseed oil is a natural antimicrobial agent, making linoleum a good choice for kitchens. It lasts about 30 to 40 years, and generally costs about $4 per square foot.

• **Rubber:** Often used for play or outdoor areas where nonslip surfaces are needed, natural virgin rubber flooring is manufactured from latex, the sap of rubber trees, which typically grow in tropical areas, mostly in Asia. But rubber can also be produced synthetically. Some rubber flooring is made from recycled materials, such as rubber tires, which are abundant in North America. Rubber is chemically stable, although it does outgas slightly, giving it a distinctive smell, but emission of toxic elements is low. Because of its natural tackiness, it can be installed without adhesives, lessening its outgassing potential compared with other materials. It is also easy to clean and durable, lasting about 20 years. Rubber flooring usually is flammable, however, and can be problematic for people with allergies. It costs about $5 to $7 per square foot.

• **Carpets and rugs:** Carpets and rugs are made from many types of materials, some natural and some synthetic, so their green properties must be evaluated first by their material type. Carpets and rugs made from any kind of natural material—from wool, cotton and silk to coir, sisal and jute—are eco-friendly in that they don't outgas, unless they've been finished or dyed with toxic substances or have synthetic backings. Natural fibers have different levels of durability, however, and some, such as sisal or jute, are prone to mildew and should not be used in humid locations. Most carpet is made from petroleum-based materials, such as nylon or polyester. This type of carpet is commonly criticized for its outgassing of VOCs in the home, and binders used to make synthetic carpets and padding may outgas for years after installation, so ask your installer to unroll and air out the carpet in a well-ventilated area before installation, and ventilate to the extent that you can for 48 to 72 hours after installation. Once installed, carpeting has excellent sound- and thermal-insulating properties. But it's practically impossible to keep it truly clean. Furthermore, synthetic carpet never breaks down completely and is one of the big contributors to greenhouse gas emissions in our landfills. While carpet is the softest flooring material considered here, it is one of the least durable, and may require replacement about every 11 years. It costs from about $4 and up per square foot.

• **Vinyl:** From an eco-friendly point of view, polyvinyl chloride (PVC) flooring is simply at odds with the environment. But because it's inexpensive and easy to install, it's one of the most popular flooring choices—14 billion pounds of it are produced each year in North America. It also presents health hazards across its entire life cycle, from production and installation to use and disposal. It is a nonrenewable petroleum-based plastic, and the oil needed to make it often travels thousands of miles to get to North America, making it energy-inefficient to produce. Once it's installed, vinyl may outgas potentially harmful compounds for years. And when its useful life ends, it will not decay in landfills. However, the Vinyl Institute has claimed it is making progress in recycling the material. Available in sheets or tiles, it starts at about $2.50 per square foot.

energy conservation

Today, American homes use more electricity than ever—the amount of electricity consumed has quadrupled since 1940, powering about 200 million personal computers and an equal number of cellular phones among a multitude of other appliances and home electronics. American homes are also bigger than ever, using 21 percent more electricity today than they did in the late 1970s.

Through its Energy Star program, the U.S. government's Environmental Protection Agency has helped Americans dramatically cut greenhouse gas emissions and trim their utility bills by about one-third, saving them billions of dollars. A primary requirement for new homes to earn an Energy Star rating is to be at least 15 percent more efficient than homes built to the 2004 residential code. The program also includes guidelines for indoor air quality for new homes. The following pages outline some of the steps you can take to improve the energy efficiency of your home.

heating, ventilation and air conditioning

Heating and cooling systems account for more than half of the energy use in a typical U.S. home and can account for about $1,000 in annual costs. To reduce the energy consumption and cost of cooling and heating, the first step is to maximize your home's efficiency.

Do-It-Yourself Energy Audit
To find out if your home is wasting energy, start by conducting your own energy audit. Walk through your home and review these key areas:

• **Make note of air leaks or drafts.** By reducing drafts, you could save from 5 to 30 percent in energy costs per year and enhance your comfort at the same time. Check for gaps along baseboards or edges of the flooring and ceiling. Check for air flow around window frames, doors, fireplaces, electrical outlets, switch plates, attic hatches and air conditioners. Also look for gaps around pipes and wires. You can usually seal these leaks by caulking or weatherstripping them.

• **Inspect your heating and cooling systems annually.** If you have a forced-air furnace, check your filters and replace them as needed—generally about once every month or two, especially during periods of high usage. Have a professional check and clean your equipment once a year. If the unit is more than 15 years old, consider replacing the system with a newer, energy-efficient unit.

• **Check the insulation.** Heat loss in your home could be substantial if you have insufficient insulation. Builders generally install the amount of insulation recommended at the time your home is constructed, and if you have an older home, the level of insulation might be inadequate. Start by sealing any gaps around ductwork or pipes with an expanding foam caulk or some other permanent sealant. To check a wall's insulation level, turn off the circuit breaker for any outlets in the wall and test the outlets to be sure they're not "hot" (plug a lamp, turn the switch on to be sure it doesn't go on). Then remove the cover plate from one of the outlets and gently probe into the wall with a thin stick. If there's some resistance, you have some insulation. Alternatively, you can drill a small hole in a closet or in some other unobtrusive place to see what the wall cavity is filled with. To determine if the entire wall is insulated, or if the insulation has settled, you would need to have a professional do a thermographic inspection. If you have an attic hatch located above a finished space, check to see if it is as well insulated as the rest of the attic as well as weatherstripped. And check to see if there's a vapor barrier under the insulation, such as tar paper, kraft paper attached to batts, or plastic sheeting. If not, paint the interior ceilings with a vapor-barrier paint to limit transmission of water vapor into the space. Be sure your basement, water heater, hot water pipes and furnace ducts are insulated, too.

In addition to addressing any issues you find after doing an energy audit, control your energy consumption by turning down or turning off the heat and air conditioning when you aren't home. Try using a programmable thermostat or setting your thermostat yourself to 68 degrees while you are awake and 60 degrees while you are asleep or away from home. In the summer, keep the thermostat at 78 degrees while you are at home, but give your air conditioning a rest when you are away. This will allow you to save about 10 percent a year on your home energy costs. If every house in America did this, our total greenhouse gas production would drop by about 35 million tons of CO_2, about the equivalent of taking 6 million cars off the road.

When it's hot outside, most people instinctively turn on the AC. But air conditioners guzzle energy. To reduce energy consumption, try non-AC cooling strategies to save money and the planet. Open your windows and interior doors to allow air to flow freely through your house. Install a whole-house fan and turn it on at the end of the day,

when it begins to cool off outside. Plant deciduous trees on the south, east and west sides of your home to block the sun and keep the house cooler. And install window shades or curtains and keep them closed during the day to prevent direct sunlight from entering the house.

If you're thinking of replacing or upgrading an existing heating and cooling system, first learn about the limitations of your current system and available energy sources in your area. When choosing a system for a new house, you'll have a wider array of options.

household appliances and electronics

In the average U.S. home, appliances and home electronics account for about 20 percent of the energy bills. If you want a green home and plan to purchase new appliances, choose and use no more than you really need. Also, try to select the most energy-efficient appliance or home electronic item you can find.

Appliances: When shopping for and comparing energy-efficient appliances, always look for the yellow and black Energy Guide label, which is required by the U.S. Federal Trade Commission on most home appliances, except for stove ranges and ovens (the Energy Guide label is also not required on home electronics, such as computers, televisions and home audio equipment). These labels provide an estimate of the product's energy consumption or energy efficiency. They also show the highest and lowest energy consumption or efficiency estimates of similar appliance models. Also look for Energy Star labels, which appear on appliances and home electronics that meet strict energy-efficiency criteria established by the DOE and EPA. The Energy Star program covers most home electronics and appliances, except for water heaters, stove ranges and ovens.

From an energy perspective, your refrigerator will use much more energy than cooking appliances, since the fridge operates 24/7. As a result, cooking appliances aren't even covered by the Energy Star program or the minimum federal efficiency standards. So if you want to choose a green cooking device, your choice is really between getting one that consumes less energy to cook or one that creates less indoor air pollution.

green kitchen tips
Be healthy and energy-efficient in the kitchen by following these tips:

• **Instead of using small electronic gadgets** for chopping, grinding and mixing, perform these tasks manually.

• **Cook meals in small appliances,** like microwaves or toaster ovens, to save energy.

• **Recycle your old appliances.** Ask your power company about recycling rebates or check with your local recycling department or visit *earth911.com* to find out how to recycle appliances you plan to replace.

• **Refrigerate responsibly** and opt not to install special wine, outdoor or mini refrigerators if possible.

• **Replace a refrigerator that is more than 12 years old** with a new Energy Star–approved model. And choose a refrigerator with a freezer on top if possible. It's more efficient than a bottom-freezer model and much more efficient than a side-by-side model.

• **Avoid refrigerators with through-the-door ice and water dispensers.** They can increase energy consumption by up to 20 percent.

• **Check to be sure gas flames burn blue.** If the flames are orange, your burners probably need servicing.

Electronics: When it comes to green electronics, there are few clear-cut choices. As far as the green trade-offs between plasma versus LCDs, the prevailing wisdom is that you'll save electricity most of the time by buying an LCD—though you'll spend more on the initial purchase. You will also save power if you unplug it from the wall when you're not using it. The same holds true for any electronic device, as the cord draws what's known as a "phantom load," or small amount of power even if the device is not activated.

A lot of personal computers now come with a power-down or sleep mode feature for the CPU and monitor. Energy Star–qualified computers power down to a sleep mode that consumes 15 watts or less power—about 70 percent less electricity than a computer without power management features. Energy Star–rated monitors can power down into two successive sleep modes, one more efficient than the other. Also, be aware that screen savers are not energy savers—and in fact can use more energy than not using one. For energy savings and convenience, turn off the monitor if you aren't going to use your computer for more than 20 minutes and turn off both the CPU and monitor if you're not going to use your computer for more than two hours. For more efficiency, be sure your monitors, printers and other accessories are on a power strip/surge protector. When this equipment is not in use for extended periods, turn off the switch on the power strip to prevent them from drawing power even when shut off.

To cut related annual energy expenses by 30 percent, choose Energy Star–labeled computers, printers, scanners, copiers, fax machines, lighting, cordless phones, answering machines and audio equipment.

it is needed, meaning it doesn't produce the standby energy losses associated with storage water heaters, which can save you money. For homes that use 41 gallons or fewer of hot water daily, demand water heaters can be 24 to 34 percent more energy-efficient than storage tank heaters. They can be 8 to 14 percent more energy-efficient for large-family households that use a lot of hot water—around 86 gallons per day.

lighting

Artificial lighting also consumes energy—almost 15 percent of a household's electricity use. The good news is that new fixtures, bulbs and lighting controls can reduce lighting energy use in homes by up to 75 percent. To reduce energy consumed by lighting, many people have switched from standard incandescent bulbs to more efficient compact fluorescents, but there are other energy-efficient light sources to choose from. Here's a rundown of their characteristics, lifespan and costs:

• **Standard incandescent:** The most common bulb used in residential applications, incandescents provide a warm, consistent light. They are inexpensive but not energy-efficient.
Cost: 75¢ per bulb
Lifespan: 750–2,500 hours

• **Compact fluorescent:** These bulbs use 33 to 80 percent less electricity than an incandescent yet last up to 10 times longer without sacrificing the amount of light. They have a reputation for offering cool and diffuse light, but have been improved in recent years to provide more appealing light resembling incandescent or natural light.
Cost: $2.50 per bulb
Lifespan: Up to 10,000 hours

water heaters

Heating water can account for 14 to 25 percent of the energy consumed in your home. You can reduce your monthly water heating bills by selecting the appropriate water heater for your home and by using some energy-efficient water heating strategies. If you plan to buy a new water heater, or replace an existing one, choose a system that not only will provide enough hot water but will do so energy-efficiently, saving you money.

One of the most efficient options is a demand (tankless or instantaneous) water heater. This type of system provides hot water only as

Energy Efficiency Resources

• *ftc.gov/bcp/conline/edcams/ eande/index.html:* For access to the government's Energy Guide and energy-use data for various appliances.
• *efficientproducts.org:* For good research on energy-efficient appliances and electronics.
• *getenergyactive.org/wisely/ progs.pdf:* For energy-efficiency

programs and services of America's electric companies and ideas on what you can do to reduce your carbon footprint.
• *climateprotect.org:* For information on green energy solutions from the Alliance for Climate Protection.
• *ase.org:* The Alliance to Save Energy provides information on incentives for living energy efficiently.

• *naima.org:* The North American Insulation Manufacturers Association is an industry trade group that offers insight on insulation alternatives.
• *energysavers.gov:* For more information on conducting your own energy audit or hiring a professional auditor. If you're thinking of replacing your HVAC system, visit the following link to determine if

it's worthwhile to do: *energysavers. gov/your_home/space_heating_ cooling/index.cfm/mytopic=12310.*
• *eere.energy.gov:* The DOE's Energy Efficiency and Renewable Energy website offers tools that can help you decide whether to invest in a more energy-efficient appliance, determine your electricity loads or estimate any appliance energy consumption.

• **Tungsten halogen:** These efficient incandescent bulbs produce a bright, warm light and have a longer, more energy-efficient life than standard incandescent bulbs. They're not as efficient as CFLs, however. The shape of the bulb usually provides a focused conical beam of light, rather than the allover light generated by standard incandescents or CFLs.
Cost: About $4 per bulb
Lifespan: About 2,000–4,000 hours

• **Xenon and krypton:** These incandescent sources produce clear warm, white light and are very energy-efficient. Xenon bulbs come in a wide range of shapes and sizes with a variety of bases for different applications, including under-cabinet strips.
Cost: About $4 per bulb
Lifespan: About 10,000 hours

• **LED:** Light-emitting diode bulbs provide a bright, clear light, and some industry professionals believe that as technology improves, they will eventually replace CFLs and incandescent bulbs because of their extreme efficiency and long life—they last between 50 and 100 times longer than a standard incandescent (more than 20 years) and three times longer than a CFL. The newest versions are beginning to resolve the problem of color rendering ability that has limited their use to mostly decorative accent light.
Cost: $15–$100 per bulb
Lifespan: 20,000–100,000 hours

◉ *Tip: The latest breakthrough in energy-efficient bulbs is GE's new Energy-Smart LED. The super-energy-efficient 9-watt bulb generates the same amount of light as a 40-watt incandescent with 77 percent less power. It also produces the same omnidirectional quality of white light as an incandescent, unlike earlier incarnations of LEDs, which shed a cone of light in only one direction. The bulb is available through the company's website for $50 apiece. If the price seems steep, consider GE's claim that the bulb will save $85 in energy costs over the life of the bulb. Visit* gelighting.com/na/energysmartLED.

water conservation

With rising energy prices and concern about greenhouse gases, most people try to conserve energy. But we're also stretching our available water supplies to the limits—public demand for water has more than tripled since 1950, and Americans now use an average of 100 gallons of water each day. This increased demand threatens both human health and the environment: A recent government survey showed that at least 36 states are anticipating local, regional or statewide water shortages by 2013.

Most people in North America use 50 to 70 gallons of water indoors each day and about the same amount outdoors, depending on the season. Indoors, about 75 percent of an average household's water usage occurs in the bathroom, and the toilet accounts for about 28 percent of that water use.

Thankfully, manufacturers of household fixtures, fittings and appliances that use, condition or process water are creating more sophisticated, energy-efficient, conservation-oriented products than ever before. Furthermore, the Environmental Protection Agency's WaterSense program now makes it easier to identify water-efficient products and practices so that we can help preserve water supplies for future generations, while saving money and protecting the environment at the same time. If every household in America installed a WaterSense-labeled faucet or aerator, we could save more than 60 billion gallons of water each year. Doing so would also help us save money on water bills. To get a sense of the energy consumed by your personal water usage, running your faucet for five minutes uses about as much energy as letting a 60-watt lightbulb run for 14 hours.

simple steps to save water

Aside from replacing water-guzzling appliances, fixtures and fittings with efficient models, try these other simple steps for conserving water:

• **Fix all leaks.** A leaky faucet, dripping at a rate of one drip per second, can waste more than 3,000 gallons of water each year. One leaky toilet can waste about 200 gallons of water a day. To check for leaks in general, read your water meter before and after a two-hour period when no water is being used. If the meter doesn't read exactly the same, you probably have a leak.

• **Shower rather than bathe.** A full bathtub requires about 70 gallons of water, while taking a five-minute shower uses just 10 to 25 gallons. Limit your showers to the time it takes to soap up, wash down and rinse off.

• **Water the garden wisely.** A typical single-family suburban household uses at least 30 percent of its water outdoors for irrigation. Some experts estimate that more than 50 percent of landscape water use goes to waste due to evaporation or runoff from overwatering. Drip irrigation systems use between 20 and 50 percent less water than conventional in-ground sprinkler systems.

- **Control your faucet.** The average bathroom faucet flows at a rate of 2 gallons per minute. If you turn off the tap while brushing your teeth or shaving, you can save up to 8 gallons of water per day, or 240 gallons a month.

- **Fill it up.** The average standard washing machine uses about 41 gallons of water per load. High-efficiency washing machines use fewer than 28 gallons of water per load. To achieve even greater savings, wash only full loads of laundry or use the appropriate load size selection on the washing machine.

- **Don't flush money away.** If your toilet was made in 1992 or earlier, you probably have an inefficient model that uses at least 3.5 gallons per flush. New and improved high-efficiency models use less than 1.3 gallons per flush. Compared to an inefficient toilet, a WaterSense-labeled toilet could save a family of four more than $90 annually on their water bill, and $2,000 over the lifetime of the toilet. Alternatively, you can upgrade an old toilet more affordably by replacing the flush mechanism with a dual-flush toilet valve kit. One company that makes them is Flush Choice, and they're available for around $60 at Green Depot stores.

- **Install water-saving showerheads and low-flow faucet aerators.** Inexpensive water-saving showerheads or restrictors are easy to install. For less than $15, you can install one of these yourself and save up to 500 gallons per year.

- **Wash wisely.** In addition to fully loading dishwashers for optimum water conservation, avoid prerinsing dishes to save water, and if possible, do not wash dishes by hand. The water in a sink doesn't get hot enough to kill bacteria and leaving water running for rinsing wastes water.

Water-Saving Resources

For more water saving strategies, check out these sources:
- *epa.gov/watersense*: The EPA's WaterSense program.
- *eartheasy.com*: Information, tips and product ideas that support sustainable living.
- *wateruseitwisely.com*: For a hundred-plus ways to conserve water in your area and info on how to contact your water authority.
- *energysavers.gov/your_home/water_heating*: The U.S. DOE's Energy Efficiency and Renewable Energy site, with tips on how to lower your water-heating bills.

eco-friendly decorating

A lot of furniture is like a lot of standard houses: It's made with toxic materials and finishes, and fabricated and transported in wasteful, inefficient ways that pollute the environment. Today, however, many responsible makers of home furnishings are producing sustainable products and operating with sustainable practices. Furthermore, interested organizations are doing their part to create industry-specific standards for evaluating the environmental impact of home furnishings products and manufacturing processes, making it easier for consumers to understand just how green their home goods choices really are.

Identifying Certified Sustainable Furniture

To help clarify and define standards for sustainable design for furnishings manufacturers, designers, retailers and consumers alike, two organizations have recently developed guidelines and certification programs specifically for the furniture industry. One organization is the American Home Furnishings Alliance. Its voluntary Enhancing Furniture's Environmental Culture (EFEC) system helps registered companies analyze the environmental impact of their processes, materials and products on a facility-by-facility basis. To complement this effort, the Alliance also established a more comprehensive Sustainable By Design certification program.

Among the furniture companies with facilities that have passed the EFEC audit are four of the top 25 furniture sources for the U.S.: La-Z-Boy, which is also the parent company of American Drew, Kincaid and Lea Industries; Flexsteel Industries, which includes DMI; Hooker Furniture, which includes the Sam Moore and Bradington-Young upholstery divisions; and Bassett Furniture. Two other top companies, Franklin and Leggett & Platt Consumer Products Unit, have facilities that are expected to complete the program as well. Another large furniture group known as Furniture Brands International recently announced that facilities operated by companies under its umbrella, including Lane, Thomasville, Broyhill, Henredon, Drexel Heritage, Maitland-Smith, Pearson and Laneventure, will also implement the EFEC program, and one of its companies, Hickory Chair, has already completed EFEC registration. Along with these top sources, five additional furniture companies—Century Furniture, C.R. Laine, Fairfield Chair, Vaughan-Bassett and Craftmaster's upholstery division—have also completed EFEC registration. Of these companies, C.R. Laine, Hickory Chair, Kincaid, American Drew and Lea Industries have achieved Sustainable By Design designation.

The other organization involved in establishing standards in the

Furnishings from C.R. Laine, such as this plush sofa, tufted ottoman and wing chairs, are made in America and meet the standards of both green certification programs established by the American Home Furnishings Alliance.

home furnishings industry is the Sustainable Furnishings Council, a nonprofit industry association founded in 2006 that includes more than 400 members, including manufacturers, retailers, environmental organizations, designers and individuals. Known for insisting on rigorous compliance with established sustainability standards, the organization launched a public advertising and in-store tagging program that enables consumers to identify retailers and products that meet or exceed its sustainability standards.

To encourage and acknowledge sustainable design and business practices in the home furnishings industry even more, the AHFA, in conjunction with Cargill BiOH polyols, launched the Sage Awards program in 2008. The program seeks to discover and recognize industry innovators in the realm of green design and business practices, and finalists in the first two programs were Cisco Brothers, Hickory Chair, Valley Forge Fabrics, Century Furniture, Copeland Furniture and La-Z-Boy. Among the companies who participated in the 2010 program are Columbia Forest Products, Flexsteel Industries, Lazar,

Good Green Furniture Resources

Several manufacturers of upholstered seating are producing various eco-friendly options. Here are a few favorites:

• **Cisco Brothers**, an industry leader in sustainable and eco-friendly furniture, makes its pieces using the highest quality-natural materials, such as soy-based foam, nontoxic glues and FSC-certified woods. *ciscobrothers.com*.

• **Rowe Furniture**, a founding member of the Sustainable Furnishings Council, recently launched its EcoRowe initiative, which includes eco-friendly manufacturing processes, eco-cushion cores, natural fiber fabrics, and several certified organic cotton fabrics finished with an eco-wash process that uses biodegradable solvents to prevent color migration. *rowefurniture.com*.

• **Lee Industries** offers earth-friendly naturalLEE furniture, which includes FSC- and SFI-certified wood frames, soy-based cushions, and water-based finishes. *leeindustries.com*.

• **Mitchell Gold** produces upholstered furniture and case goods with a commitment to eco-friendliness. The company's cushions are wrapped in 80 percent regenerated fibers with cushions composed of 10 percent soy. Most of its frames and case goods are made from wood from domestic suppliers dedicated to responsible forest management and eco-friendly parawood solids. *mgbwhome.com*.

This sleigh bed and table from Kincaid is made from sustainably harvested pine and coated with an eco-friendly finish.

the Phillips Collection, Revco International, TLS by Design and Zenda Leather, which was the winner of the award. If you purchase furniture made by any of these companies, you can be sure that yours will be among the most sustainable furnishings made today.

In addition to these organizations, some of the trustworthy certifiers of building products, such as Greenguard, the Forest Stewardship Council and the Sustainable Forestry Initiative, can also be resources for more information on green furnishings. Many companies also make claims about their furniture's sustainability and may in fact be using green materials and practicing green manufacturing methods but not be certified. If you want to purchase furniture that doesn't meet the criteria of these programs, then you'll need to inquire about how the manufacturer verifies its sustainability efforts and then make your own judgment about its eco-friendliness.

From a sustainability perspective, the greenest choice you can make regarding furniture is to continue to use, recycle or repurpose existing furnishings if they're still viable. Antiques and vintage furnishings are not only green, they can also increase in value over time. Estate sales, auctions, antiques shops and other stores and shows offering antique and vintage furniture are great sources for high-quality furniture. Or check out flea markets and tag sales for affordable furniture finds.

mattresses and bedding

The bedroom is the place where we rest and regenerate. As we sleep, our bodies shed metabolic waste and restore our natural electrical systems and internal organs. We also spend at least one-third of our lives in bed. So if you have to pick and choose, your bed and bedding should be the first green furnishings purchases you make for your home.

- **Mattresses:** The materials in many mattresses, including polyurethane foam, synthetic fabrics, chemical fire retardants, toxic dyes, formaldehyde, anti-fungicides, pesticide-treated cotton and stain-resistant chemicals, can cause allergic reactions and other health problems. In response to consumers' concerns about the harmful effects these chemicals may impose, many manufacturers have begun to produce healthier or organic mattresses. These mattresses are often made with a combination of certified organic cotton, natural latex and wool, and do not include metal springs, which conduct electricity that can disturb our equilibrium. (Because metal attracts electromagnetic fields that can interfere with our bodies' natural electrical systems, you may want to choose wood bed frames in lieu of metal ones, too.)

Eco-Friendly vs. Organic Mattresses

To be helpful in terms of fire-resistance and moisture-wicking, a mattress should be topped with at least 2.2 lbs of wool, and an all-natural cotton cover or aloe-vera ticking. Some organic mattresses contain up to 8 lbs of compressed organic wool on top to wick away moisture. More affordable mattresses include about 65 percent natural materials. Some of these mattresses have a 2" layer of Talalay natural latex, atop a 5" plant-based foam core, which is made from a mix of soy or castor oil and petroleum.

The best plant-based polyfoam that can be made at this time is about 30 percent natural and the rest is petroleum, but manufacturers are currently working toward a 50-50 mix. Although there is petroleum in the polyfoam portion of the mattress, it is manufactured so that it doesn't outgas toxic VOCs.

Natural latex foam mattresses come in two varieties: Talalay and Dunlop. The latex in both versions comes from the sap from rubber trees. The difference is in the way they're manufactured and converted into foam. Both are good, but Talalay is a little springier and lasts a little longer.

Good Green Mattress Sources

- **Organic Mattresses Inc. (OMI):** This company's OrganicPedic line of mattresses are the purest organic mattresses currently manufactured, according to its president, Walt Bader. While great for anyone, these mattresses are ideal for people with a condition known as multiple chemical sensitivity. Visit omimattress.com.

- **Coco-Mat:** Offers mattresses made of 100 percent natural materials—natural rubber, horse and camel hair, coco fiber, linen, goose down, cactus fiber, seaweed, wool, cotton and silk—derived from sustainable sources. Visit coco-mat.com.

- **NaturaWorld:** Offers eco-friendly and organic mattresses and pillows priced to suit a range of budgets. Visit naturaworld.com.

- **Lifekind:** A California-based company that offers organic mattresses made with standards close to those of OMI. Visit lifekind.com.

Potted plants and flowers enhance
air quality indoors and out by
consuming carbon dioxide and
VOCs and releasing oxygen as a
byproduct into the atmosphere.

Natural latex provides a comfortable surface that molds to a body's contours and can last up to 20 years without sagging. But if you have sensitivities to latex, be sure to test any mattress containing this material before buying, since most mattresses are not returnable after purchase. If you're allergic to natural latex, you can find inner-spring mattresses covered with wool and cotton. Compressed wool is naturally fire-resistant, repels mites, mold and mildew, and wicks away moisture (we all lose about a pint of water each night through perspiration and breathing). For the small number of people who are severely allergic to wool, a 100 percent latex mattress may provide a healthier alternative.

To verify a manufacturer's green claims about a mattress, consumers should find out whether the product is certified by an authorized program or organization. In 2006, Greenguard certified the first bedding products for low chemical emissions and therefore is a good place to start. Or check the website of any company you're considering buying a mattress from for icons of the organizations that have certified its products.

Bedding and pillows: If you go the organic mattress route, don't forget to get an organic pillow, too. Some are made with organic wool, which wicks away moisture that causes chills and overheating. They're also antimicrobial and allergen- and bacteria-resistant to help keep nighttime sniffles at bay.

Bedding and pillows made of natural materials, such as cotton, silk, linen, wool or cotton flannel, are the best green options. But for chemically sensitive people, even natural bedding elements can pose certain health hazards. Unless they're made of certified organic natural cotton, all-cotton sheets may contain pesticide residue and emit VOCs from synthetic dyes and permanent-press finishes. Wool blankets, on the other hand, may be treated with moth-proof finishes. The greenest bedding is made of undyed, certified organic fabrics.

If you have asthma or allergies, buy a pillow that minimizes these issues and is certified by a credible association, such as the Asthma and Allergy Foundation of America, which, before certifying their products, puts them through a stringent scientific testing process.

plants and flowers

Many people know that trees and plants enhance the quality of the air outdoors by consuming carbon dioxide, converting it into food for themselves and releasing oxygen as a byproduct into the atmosphere. But plants bring eco-friendly benefits to indoor spaces, too. Recent research from the University of Georgia shows that certain plants are extremely effective at removing harmful VOCs from indoor air, which means they can play a critical role in improving the healthiness of your home.

Five "super-ornamentals" scored especially high in removing contaminants from the air through a process called phytoremediation. These include the purple waffle plant (*Hemigraphis alternata*), English ivy (*Hedera helix*), variegated wax plant (*Hoya carnosa*), asparagus fern (*Asparagus densiflorus*) and the purple heart plant (*Tradescantia pallida*). The purple waffle plant is the real star among the super-ornamentals.

If you don't have a green thumb, start by introducing just one plant into your home, and it'll go a long way toward making your home healthier and greener in both senses of the word.

Access to views of water, ideally to the south of one's home, is auspicious from a *feng shui* perspective. Winding river views are seen as especially beneficial, bestowing positive *ch'i*, or energy, on the property of anyone who has direct access to it. For *feng shui* practitioners, the element of water is often associated with wealth.

spirit

When shaping a home, it's easy to get caught up in the material things that make a room look good. But just as important are the intangibles that make a space feel good. For your home is much more than a reflection of your taste and lifestyle. It also influences how you think and feel and act. And this connection between our spaces and our frame of mind is the spirit of the home. The relationship between our environments and our wellbeing has been observed and cultivated by different cultures in different ways for thousands of years.

According to *feng shui*, the ideal location for a home is halfway up a hill, shielded by trees and nestled into the landscape. Like rivers, passageways leading to the entrance are considered more hospitable if they gently wind toward the door rather than lead straight to it.

In the East, practitioners of *feng shui*, the Chinese art of placement, use a variety of tools and techniques to correct imbalances in what they call *ch'i*, or universal energy. Similarly, experts in *vastu shastra*, an ancient Indian system of constructing and organizing built environments, offer prescriptions for harmoniously aligning dwellings with nature. In Japan, a philosophy known as *wabi-sabi*, which is intimately tied to Zen Buddhism, has for centuries attuned its followers to the art of finding beauty in the imperfection of nature and using it as a guide to cultivating living spaces that reflect a spiritual outlook. In the West, the Egyptians, and later the Greeks, developed a system of sacred geometry, which they employed in the construction of structures like the pyramids and the Parthenon. And variations on this system inspired the construction of many European cathedrals in later centuries.

But for much of the 20th century in the Western world, the connection between our inner and outer worlds was forgotten. Practitioners of age-old building traditions as well as scientists and doctors have blamed that disconnect for all sorts of maladies, from seasonal affective disorder (SAD) to insomnia to multiple chemical sensitivity syndrome (MCS). Over the past 20 years, however, a resurgence of interest in these ancient building philosophies has sparked a renewed interest in cultivating spaces that connect us more deeply with nature and the cosmos. The growth of the green movement and the sciences of industrial psychology and environmental-behavioral dynamics have produced evidence that reinforces many of the benefits said to emerge from age-old systems like these.

Designing with spirit is about connecting to the grander scheme of nature and universal energy. Yet it is also about creating spaces that are deeply personal—in harmony with who you are and what you need on an individual level. The ideas embodied in a few of these ancient Asian schools of thought may help you open the door to more consciously creating a home that is in tune with the subtler forces of nature. And so, the essence of some of these philosophies is outlined on the pages that follow. While many of the concepts of *feng shui* and *vastu* are rooted in science and reason, others are esoteric and often criticized as superstitious. Yet followers of these traditions often value the esoteric prescriptions for their ability to inspire helpful actions through the power of symbolism, as any spiritual ritual intends to do. And for those who remain doubtful, there are plenty of *feng shui* and *vastu* prescriptions, such as clearing clutter or introducing plants, that bring practical and aesthetic benefits to a room that even the staunchest of skeptics cannot deny.

Throughout history, philosophers, poets and social scientists in all parts of the world have also pondered the spirit of the home—and the following pages offer a glance at some ideas of a few contemporary thinkers in these realms, too.

feng shui

To the Chinese, a person's well-being and fortune is often attributed less to individual actions than to the mysterious forces of nature. These elemental forces are known as *feng shui*, which literally means "wind and water," and are believed to affect a person's business, family, reputation and health. Although the practice of *feng shui* is surrounded with mystery, many of its precepts are the result of centuries of scientific observation of the ways in which people are affected, for better or worse, by their surroundings. And the goal of *feng shui* is to improve the quality of one's life by creating spaces and arranging furniture in ways that harmonize with nature and cosmic currents of energy known as *ch'i*.

The practice of *feng shui* is actually part science and part art, encompassing ecology, geography, geomancy, astronomy, divination, folklore, astrology, numerology and other natural and "psychic" aspects. The Chinese see a mystical link between people and their surroundings and recognize the role humans play in a universe that they regard as a sacred metabolic system. To enhance their prosperity and improve their relations, the Chinese choose sites and build houses that enable them to harness and channel the essences of wind, water and other elements in ways that are understood to be auspicious. And when ideal conditions cannot be achieved, they deploy antidotes or cures to the areas of the landscape or built space that disrupt the smooth flow of *ch'i*.

landscape

Symbols and shapes: *Feng shui* relies heavily on symbols, and many of the images that play a role in the evaluation of sites and buildings relate to real or mythological animals, such as tigers, turtles, phoenixes and dragons. Geomancers often survey the shapes of the landscape around a home for their resemblance to certain animals, which can be deemed either protective or harmful to a home on a property depending on their location in relation to the structure.

Location: According to *feng shui*, the best location for a house is in a commanding but sheltered position halfway up a hill or mountain. A house positioned on either the south or east side of a hill or mountain is more auspicious than one situated on the north or west. These prescriptions have a practical foundation. Instead of being shrouded in the shade and buffeted by the winds of the north or blasted with the harsh light of the setting sun in the west, a home that faces south or east will have access to the gentle warmth and softer light of the rising sun and benefit from conditions in which vegetation can prosper. A view of a body of water or a river to the south, in particular one with

Right: Doors, which are seen as mouths to the home, are crucial to the *feng shui* of a house. To invite in wholesome *ch'i* they should be well maintained and free of clutter to ease access into and out of the home. Flanking a door with plants and lighting is said to brighten the *ch'i* entering a home.

Opposite: Unlike furniture arrangements in many Western rooms, which revolve around a focal point such as a television or a view, *feng shui* furniture arrangements in living rooms position chairs occupied by the dominant adults in the house to have a commanding view of the primary entrance.

gentle irregular contours, is also considered beneficial. Water often represents money to *feng shui* practitioners, and straight rivers are seen as harmful, threatening to wash one's riches away, while rivers with curves gently disperse beneficial *ch'i* to the surrounding areas.

Conservation: With respect to the landscape, many of the recommendations of *feng shui* practitioners align with those of eco-conscious architects, builders and conservationists in the West. For example, houses are positioned and constructed to maximize the natural arc of the sun and provide the most hospitable exposures to daylight. Alterations to the landscape are minimized—piercing the earth's surface, diverting the flow of water and disturbing nature's balance is avoided whenever possible. Trees are also preserved whenever possible or planted to prevent soil erosion and buffer wind.

houses

Shape: As they do with topographical features and plots of land, *feng shui* masters evaluate the shapes of houses and rooms—some of which are more auspicious than others. From a *feng shui* perspective, ideal homes are built in square or rectangular shapes, where *ch'i* is free to flow easily. The same is true for the shapes of rooms. If a house is shaped like a boot, for example, or a cleaver, *feng shui* masters recommend situating important rooms, such as master bedrooms or living rooms, away from the walls that form the sole of a boot shape, where a person's *ch'i* might feel crushed or demoralized, or along the blade edge of the cleaver, where one's *ch'i* might feel on edge or endangered.

Another common problem in need of a cure is what some *feng shui* masters refer to as a hollow or void, places where the smooth line of a wall is obstructed by an indentation that notches into the square or rectangular shape of a house or room and thereby hinders the flow of energy into these areas. A similar but opposite problem is an extension or protrusion in a wall that disrupts the clean geometric shape of a house or room. These areas distort the energy of any sector they occupy and create an imbalance. Spaces, columns or other built-in elements with sharp angles or oblique lines pose another problem in houses and rooms. They produce what *feng shui* experts call cutting or killing *ch'i*, a sharp, knifelike energy that can be harmful to anyone perched in its path.

Architectural elements: Architectural features, such as doors and windows, staircases and light fixtures, also play a critical role in the *feng shui* of a home, as they are seen to be analogous to the sense organs of the human body. Doors are seen as the mouths of a home, where life-enhancing *ch'i* enters and nourishes the occupants. Windows, too,

are like mouths, eyes or noses that take in views and allow *ch'i* to flow like breath through various spaces and to the outdoors. Ideally, doors should be in proportion to the house, and the entrance should be expansive and light to engender a sense of expansiveness and joy. Small doors can stifle the flow of *ch'i* and cramped entrances can make its occupants feel depressed or timid. An entrance should also be free of obstacles to allow the smooth flow of *ch'i* into a room. However, too much *ch'i* can also be problematic, so the Chinese often place a screen or a wind chime along a passage, or in rooms arranged *en enfilade*, to slow the flow of *ch'i* through areas where it has the potential to shoot through like an arrow.

The direction in which the door faces can also impact destiny. Doors facing north, for example, bring good fortune in business, while doors facing south bring fame. East-facing doors support a good family life, while doors looking west bring fame to children. The best windows are those that open completely outward, like French doors to the outside to allow an unrestricted flow of *ch'i*. And ideally, windows should not outnumber doors by more than three to one, or children will quarrel and fight with their parents (windows are said to represent the mouths of children and doors the mouths of parents).

One way to remedy this problem is to hang a bell or wind chime over the door to enhance the *ch'i* that flows in as the door opens.

The position of the entrance and overhead beams are also seen as problematic to *feng shui* masters, especially when positioned over key pieces of furniture, such as a bed or dining table, where they are believed to suppress the *ch'i* of a room as well as that of an individual sitting or lying beneath them, and put a damper on growth and prosperity. And staircases and light fixtures are key in ensuring the easy circulation of *ch'i*. Like rivers, the best stairs should gently curve as they wind up, rather than shoot straight down toward a door, where beneficial *ch'i* could literally fly out the door. Stairs should also be free of clutter and unconfined by low ceilings to enable the smooth flow of *ch'i*. In halls or areas with low ceilings, light fixtures can brighten and improve *ch'i*.

Room placement and furniture arrangement: The position of rooms relative to the front entrance as well as to each other also affects *feng shui*. Experts say that front doors should never open directly onto a bathroom, for example, where water plays an important role. The Chinese often equate water with money, and if the *ch'i* that enters the home flows directly into the bathroom, it's like flushing money away. Kitchens and dining rooms should be placed near each other but ideally not be the first thing people see when they enter, or guests will eat and run.

The placement of furniture can also either help or hinder the smooth flow of *ch'i* within a room. In living rooms, for example, the head of the household's chair should face the door. Similarly, desks in dens or home offices should always be positioned to have a commanding view of the door catercorner from the line of the entrance. The ideal position for a bed is also catercorner to the door. These positions allow the occupant to clearly see anyone coming through the door without getting startled. The direction in which a bed faces also influences the destiny of the occupants and will enhance the life area in which the bed points.

Color: Color also plays a key role in enhancing the *feng shui* of various rooms. *Feng shui* masters have ways of associating different segments of a home with different aspects of life, such as health, wealth and relationships, and different auspicious colors can enhance the *feng shui* of each area. Each area is generally associated with groups of colors,

Based on advice from a *feng shui* consultant, may husband and I painted the interior of a coat closet on the north side of our home with a deep blue paint from Benjamin Moore. We also incorporated new Pax organizing units from Ikea to keep the space clutter-free and well organized to enhance the *ch'i* of the space.

earth, fire, water and metal—all of which are seen as manifestations of *ch'i*. Each of these elements is, in turn, associated with different seasons, cardinal directions and colors, as well as aspects of human nature. Wood, for example, represents kindness and loyalty, while metal stands for righteousness and fastidiousness. In evaluating a space, *feng shui* masters look not only at the physical attributes of a room, but at the qualities that may dominate or appear to be lacking in a person, and aim to correct any imbalances. One of each of the five elements feeds or "gives birth" to the others, and in true yin-yang fashion, one of each also destroys another. In my own kitchen, for example, Atsushi Shono, a Japanese *feng shui* master I consulted, noticed the sink was directly across from the stove. "Water kills fire," he told me. "But water feeds wood, and wood feeds fire." To improve the *feng shui* of our kitchen, he suggested placing a plant between the sink and the stove. I followed his advice until we renovated the kitchen. In the new plan, I made a point of moving the sink out of alignment with the stove.

mysticism

Names, numbers and astrology: Subtler aspects in the evaluation of the *feng shui* of a place are the names, birthdates and astrological signs of the occupants of a home. In his analysis of our home, for example, Shono asked my husband and me for the exact spelling of our full names, as well as our birthdates and address (house number), to determine the quality of *ch'i* of our home (known in the Japanese form of *feng shui* as *taku-ki* fate), as well as our personal *ch'i* or innate energetic magnetism (known as *honmeika* fate). This helped him identify the good and bad areas of our home and how to balance them, as well as determine auspicious colors and stones for our personalities. As it turned out, my husband and I share

such as purple and gold for the wealth area of a home, or black and blue for the career area.

Elements: *Feng shui* aims to improve a person's fate by aligning their dwellings with nature. And so, elements of nature factor heavily into the mix a *feng shui* master makes to improve someone's destiny. When creating a space, the Chinese consider five elements—wood,

How to Use a Feng Shui Bagua

The *feng shui bagua* maps the way in which *ch'i*, or cosmic energy, moves within a home or room. The *bagua* also aims to help you see how your home is an extension of yourself. The instructions that follow show you how to lay out the

bagua over the floor plan of your home, so that you can identify which rooms are located in the different areas of your life and make changes or improvements in ways that suit your goals.

1. Draw a precise floor plan outline of your home (or your room, yard or office).

2. Position the plan so that the wall containing the primary entrance of the home (or space) is at the bottom of the page.
3. Draw the *bagua* map over the whole plan (all parts of your entire home or the specific room you're examining should be inside the map). If your home or room is a square or rectangular shape, the

map will lie right on the walls of the floor plan. If your space is shaped like an "L" or some other unusual shape, stretch the map over all spaces—some areas of the bagua will be outside of your space. These are not lost spaces, but they will require special attention with specific *feng shui* cures applied to remedy problem areas.

Breaking Down the Bagua

Here is a summary of the classical *feng shui bagua*. Each of the nine *feng shui guas* is associated with a direction/location, a *feng shui* element, a *feng shui* color, a *feng shui* number and life area. Different *feng shui* schools of thought associate variations of the major life areas or shades of colors to the different *guas*. Those listed below are most common.

Direction: Southeast or Rear Left
Feng shui element: Wood
Colors: Purple, Gold and Green
Life area: Wealth and Prosperity
Number: 4

The wealth area of the *bagua* is about creating material wealth. But it also affects your sense of inner abundance and blessings. If you have problems with money or generally experience bad luck, evaluate and enhance this area of your home.

Direction: South or Rear Middle
Feng shui element: Fire
Colors: Red, Orange, Purple and Bright Yellow
Life area: Fame and Reputation
Number: 9

The fame and reputation area of the *bagua* relates to how you perceive yourself, what you aspire to and where you want to be in life. Fame and aspiration also relates to issues of self-esteem and social standing. If you don't feel confident or good about yourself concentrate on improving this area. Balancing the energy here will bring inspiration, clarify your vision and enhance spiritual awareness.

Direction: Southwest or Rear Right
Feng shui element: Earth
Colors: Pink, White, Earth or Skin Tones
Life area: Relationships and Marriage
Number: 2

The *bagua*'s relationship area relates to your primary relationship with your sexual partner as well as the relationships you have with friends, family, yourself and others. If you're single or experiencing marital problems, concentrate on this area.

Direction: East or Middle Left
Feng shui element: Wood
Colors: Brown, Green and Blue
Life area: Family
Number: 3

The family and ancestors area of the *bagua* relates to your immediate family, ancestors and superiors—all of whom may support you and give you a solid foundation from which to operate. This is the area to enhance if you have family quarrels or parent issues.

Direction: Center
Feng shui element: Earth
Colors: Yellows and Earth Tones
Life area: Health
Number: 5

The center of the Bagua is Earth, which signifies You. This area affects health issues and whether you feel energized and balanced. If you feel overwhelmed, stressed or lacking in vitality, concentrate on this area. Our health is at the core of our ability to function well, so the health sector sits at the center of the bagua, affecting all other areas.

Direction: West or Middle Right
Feng shui element: Metal
Colors: White, Pastels, Silver and Gray
Life area: Creativity and Children
Number: 7

Children are the ultimate expression of creativity, but this area also influences creativity in general. If you're having problems conceiving or if your children are unhappy, focus on enhancing this area. Creativity also relates to personal self expression—whether through sport, crafts or other hobbies. This area also affects your ability to materialize what you want in life.

Direction: Northeast or Front Left
Feng shui element: Earth
Colors: Beige, Light Yellow, and Sand/Earth-colored
Life area: Knowledge, Education and Spiritual Growth
Number: 8

The area of study, knowledge and meditation is the ideal place to retreat to when you need to recharge or study. Develop this area if you feel harassed and short on time for yourself.

Direction: North or Front Middle
Feng shui element: Water
Colors: Dark Blue and Black
Life area: Career
Number: 1

The career area of the *feng shui bagua* relates to how you earn a living and your life path. The idea is that if you are on the correct path, things will seem easy and you'll feel enthusiastic and confident about your work. Cultivate this area if you are having problems at work or can't decide on your next career move.

Direction: Northwest or Front Right
Feng shui element: Metal
Colors: White, Black and Gray
Life area: Helpful People, Inspiration, Travel
Number: 6

The helpful friends, travel and inspiration area revolves around your support system in life. It also relates to how much you give of yourself. It's believed that if you give of yourself (emotionally and spiritually), you'll also find support when you need it. Another facet of this area is its connection to travel and overseas opportunities.

The wall that contains the main entrance should be oriented along the bottom of the bagua

the same *honmeika* fate, which Shono says is very rare. The good news for us is that we also share the same lucky colors and stones—no conflict!

Tools: There are several schools of *feng shui*, each with different approaches to evaluating spaces and solving problems. But all rely on various tools to ascertain the auspiciousness of a site or home. Among these tools are various types of *feng shui* compasses, a *feng shui* measurement ruler, and an octagonal template or map known as a *bagua* (which means "eight areas"). The *bagua* is actually divided into nine quadrants (eight around all four sides and one in the middle), and each is associated with a different area of one's life. This map is also referred to as a *lo shu* square, which is also divided into sections and would look like a *bagua* if you sliced off its corners.

When the bagua is placed over the floor plan of a home, a *feng shui* expert can identify the rooms associated with each life area, and note any problem areas that may need fixing to improve a person's life. Each of the nine quadrants is also associated with different colors and directions. Four of the quadrants are associated with the four cardinal directions, and these quadrants along with the central quadrant are associated with one of the five elements or manifestations of *ch'i* deemed to be auspicious for the different life areas.

Cures for problem shapes: To remedy problems in any area of the home, *feng shui* masters deploy a range of different cures. Many of these are rational and easy to understand, like positioning a room or home to take advantage of the natural course of the sun. Others use an esoteric process known as *chu-shr*, which involves rituals that are beyond the realm of rational thinking. Among the objects used to cure various problems in a room are mirrors, bamboo charcoals, gourds, bells, crystals, stones, water fountains and plants, among many others.

Simple ways to improve your home with feng shui:
• **Clear all clutter** away from the front door, inside and out.
• **Add a fountain** or an aquarium to the wealth section of your home or room. Water is believed to activate energy, especially if it's kept moving. Keep the fountain or aquarium spotlessly clean.
• **Place crystal balls** at the four corners of a void to neutralize its negative impact
• **Install lights** on either side of the front doorway, both inside and out, to brighten the *ch'i* entering your space
• **Clear any objects**, such as books or stationery, out from under your desk to keep you from feeling blocked in a home office

Consulting an Expert

As my husband and I embarked on our own home improvements, I consulted two *feng shui* masters, Atsushi Shono and Katherine Lewis, to analyze the *feng shui* of our home. Each of these masters approach *feng shui* from different schools of thought, but the suggestions they offered for improving the *feng shui* of our home did not conflict, so I incorporated ideas from both of them.

We had already committed to renovating our kitchen, which, it turns out, is located in the career area of our home. Interestingly, as we undertook the renovation, my husband and I were also shifting gears in our careers. When I spoke to Katherine Lewis, we had already begun making material decisions for the kitchen, and she promptly asked me what color they were. The floor tiles are charcoal gray and the backsplash tiles are a clear blue. Luckily, according to Lewis, these turned out to be good colors for this area, as they are the ones associated with this part of the bagua. The element of water is also associated with the area, so she suggested including something that suggested water, such as a water pitcher or an image of a river. Like Shono, Lewis also told me a sink in alignment with the stove is not auspicious from a *feng shui* perspective. So I made a point of moving the stove and sink off alignment in the revised floor plan.

Trained in several schools of *feng shui*, Lewis relies on different approaches for different circumstances. "I use the Tibetan Black Hat school if the home is already in existence, because it's simpler and more flexible," she told me. "For new projects, I use the Luo Pan Compass school." The latter approach takes physical, intractable aspects of the land into account to determine the positions of each of nine life areas. The Black Hat school relies on the bagua map. According to Lewis, all projects, large and small, involve blessing the space and honoring one's ancestors as part of the process.

vastu

Most people in the Western world are familiar with yoga, the ancient Indian science of the soul. *Yoga*, a Sanskrit word that means *unity* or *integration*, is a discipline in which various *asanas*, or physical postures, along with breathing and meditation techniques are employed to foster a sense of harmony or unity between an individual and the broader cosmos. Many Westerners are also familiar with yoga's sister science, *ayurveda*, an ancient system of healing. *Ayurveda* is actually a combination of two words: *ayur*, which means *life*, and *veda*, which means *science* or *knowledge*. But few are aware of *vastu shastra*, another ancient Indian science pertaining to architecture and design. The Sanskrit word *vastu* can be translated to mean *energy* or *imperishable substance* and also *site*, *building* or *house*. *Shastra* means *instruction*. Like yoga and *ayurveda*, *vastu* aims to promote the health of the body and spirit by guiding the design and construction of living environments in ways that are in harmony with nature's physical and metaphysical forces.

All three of these systems are included in the Hindu Vedas—a collection of writings that date back more than 5,000 years ago and describe laws of nature observed by ancient sages in all aspects of life. (Though these systems are codified in the Vedas, some scholars believe their origins can be traced back to more than 10,000 years ago and predate Hinduism and organized religion.) While each of these disciplines focuses on separate fields of study, all are also intertwined. *Vastu* is conceptually similar to *feng shui* in that it aims to harmonize the flow of energy or life force, known in Sanskrit as *prana* (like the Chinese *ch'i*), through the house. There is also wide consensus that *vastu* served as the foundation for *feng shui* and influenced the design of early structures around the globe, including the Mayan pyramids. But vastu differs from *feng shui* in many of the details, such as the directions in which various objects, rooms and materials should be placed and the colors and elements identified with certain locations.

A mixture of spiritual philosophy and science, *vastu* approaches building and design from the vantage point that everything in the universe is interconnected. Like a *feng shui* master, a *vastu* expert looks carefully at a site and chooses the best orientation for a building, aligning it with five primary elements. Slightly different from the *feng shui* elements, the *vastu* elements include space or ether, air, fire, water and earth. The idea is to harmonize a building with the environment, and with the humans who occupy it, to allow optimum vibrations to permeate the dwelling and promote health and inner peace. *Vastu* practitioners see our environments as extensions of ourselves. As such, if designed in accord with principles of *vastu*, our homes have the potential to nourish, rather than obstruct, the expression of our souls.

landscape

Symbols: Like *feng shui*, *vastu* relies on various symbols to express the subtler concepts of the practice. And like the *feng shui bagua*, a map known as a *purusha mandala* serves as an essential tool to identify the locations of certain life areas and help examine the energy of an existing or prospective building. The Sanskrit word *mandala* actually means circle, and different *mandalas*, which are used in various cultures as tools for meditation, are detailed with complex sections radiating from a central point and relate to the seen and unseen mechanisms of creation. The circular form usually overlays a square shape, which is divided into a grid of a minimum of nine additional squares that enables a structure to be analyzed for its alignment with the four cardinal directions, the energy grid of the earth and the cosmic energy of the sun.

The grid is based on the proportions of Purusha, a mythological unmanageable being who, legend has it, had to be controlled by the gods to be restrained. As a result, the image of his physique is usually compressed into a prayer-like pose, facing down with his feet together in the southwest corner and his head in the northeast. He represents archetypal cosmic male energy or pure masculine consciousness, and is contained in the square grid, which represents pure female consciousness, symbolically expressed as Mother Earth or Nature. Like the yin and yang forces of *feng shui*, the union of these opposites creates a sense of balance that is essential to the feeling of comfort and harmony in the home. As with Leonardo's Vitruvian Man, standard human proportions also influence the proportions of subdivisions of the square, which are known as *padas*.

Location: In *vastu*, nine directions are taken into consideration—the four cardinal directions of north, south, east and west as well as the intermediate directions northeast, southeast, southwest and northwest, along with the vital center from which the source of energy, or *prana*, arises. When aligned properly, a house is in harmony with the energy grid of the earth, as well as energy from the sun, moon, stars and other planets. According to *vastu* practitioners, energy flows from the center as well as along lifelines that move in alignment with the various directions and establish the house as a living organism.

Ideal orientation of a house in accord with *vastu* guidelines is in alignment with the four cardinal directions. As in *feng shui*, areas in different directions of the house are associated with various life areas that can influence the well-being of the occupants. In *vastu* tradition, east is the most auspicious direction for a house to face, as it is aligned with the life-giving, healing rays of the rising sun. The north, which is associated with health, wealth and career, also provides

nourishing cosmic energies, according to *vastu*, and *vastu* guidelines encourage placing most windows and doors in these directions. The south is identified with duty, responsibility and death, and the west corresponds to the unknown and darkness. The northeast and southwest corners of a house are considered sacred zones, with the northeast serving as the location of sacred wisdom, while the southwest is the area for rooms that nurture primary relationships. Some of the directions are also associated with various elements, colors and planets, which also influence how *prana* moves in a room.

Conservation and sustainability: As for the landscape, *vastu* practitioners advise choosing lots with a fountain or water feature to the north (the opposite of *feng shui*), and tall trees in the south. Ideally, the lot also rises slightly in the south and west to protect it from the harsher rays of the sun in these positions as it arcs through the sky. (India's location closer to the equator may have something to do with this reversal.)

In addition to positioning a structure to maximize the beneficial attributes of each direction, *vastu* also encourages the use of natural materials whenever possible, though certain natural materials are preferred over others. For example, steel and iron can interfere with the earth's electromagnetism and disrupt energy fields, and so are avoided especially in bed frames. Wood and rattan are preferred materials for furniture. Stones like granite, slate and limestone are considered acceptable as they emit a musical sound when tapped, whereas marble does not. Bricks are also acceptable, as are natural fabrics made of cotton, linen, flax, wool and silk. *Vastu* also regards certain plants, such as jasmine and basil, to be auspicious, and others, such as cacti or other thorny plants other than roses, to be inimical to humans.

houses

Shapes: To harmonize with nature, according to principles of *vastu*, ideal houses should be built in square or rectangular shapes. There are 32 different grid patterns of the *purusha mandala* that can be applied by *vastu* experts to evaluate and enhance an existing structure or create one from scratch in an ideal manner. All include *marma* points, or secret vital areas, which also align with vital centers in the human body. In the body, these points can be treated with ayurvedic acupressure to restore pranic energy. And these locations are identified in particular squares of the grid to aid in managing the design and arrangement of furniture in a home or room for the most beneficial flow of *prana*. According to *vastu*, irregularly shaped rooms or structures can cause problems for their inhabitants. As with *feng shui*, if a room has an extension or hollow or cutout area, these irregularities can cause imbalances in the affected areas and need to be rectified.

Architectural elements: *Vastu* guidelines offer recommendations on the placement of various architectural elements, and significant among them are doors. There are nine possible ideal positions for a front door on each cardinal side of a home, and only a north-facing home can benefit from a central door.

Unlike *feng shui*, *vastu* guidelines encourage a straight passage to front doors and a clear view from the front door straight through to a door or window in the back of a house. In *vastu*, open views and clear access to the outdoors are seen as beneficial, allowing *prana*, light and solar energy to fully permeate the space and nourish the environs. Such a clear path is called *vamsa danda*, or "spine of light," and enhances a room visually and energetically, keeping it from feeling stagnant. As with *feng shui*, however, overhead beams are considered oppressive, and measures should be taken, with remedies such as the introduction of *yantras* (sacred geometrical patterns), *mantras* (sacred sounds), or other symbols, stones or colors to counteract their negative effect if they can't be moved. And gently curving stairways, ideally placed on the western wall, are preferred over straight stairs.

Room placement and furniture arrangement: *Vastu* guidelines also offer specific suggestions for the placement of rooms in line with the cardinal directions and the qualities associated with each area. For example, the sacred northeast corner and zone of spiritual wisdom is associated with water and is an ideal place for a meditation room or quiet zone for reading and contemplation. It should be kept immaculately clean and clear of clutter and include a fountain, if possible, a view of clean water, such as a pool or freshwater lake or pond, or images of water. Bathrooms and kitchens should not be placed in this area. If you have one of these rooms in this location, it can be remedied with *yantras*, *mantras* or other appeasements to the proverbial gods associated with this area.

The northwest is a good place for guest rooms, as this area is associated with air and movement, and will ensure that guests will feel at ease yet not overstay their welcome. The southeast, where the fire element dominates, is the best position for a kitchen, while the southwest is optimal for the master bedroom.

Kathleen Cox, author of a book called *Vastu Living* (HarperCollins), suggests that all furnishings in any room, including the head of the bed, be set at least 4 inches from the wall to permit the free flow of *prana* throughout the home. The key *vastu* rule in the design of any building or room is that the center area, or what is known as the *Brahmasthan*, be left open to allow the space element to bring primordial energy into the room and be free to circulate obstructed. No heavy furniture or architectural elements should be placed in this

vital center. In any home, the ideal position for the tallest, heaviest pieces of furniture is in the southwest area of the home or room. This would include tall armoires in a bedroom, for example, or a refrigerator in the kitchen. The best position for the head of the bed is east, where the most beneficial cosmic rays enter a space and align a human's innate electromagnetic energy with that of the Earth. The best placement for a desk is also toward the east.

Beauty: The proper placement of furniture is one part of the *vastu* decorating equation. But beauty, known in Sanskrit as *sundari*, is another essential ingredient. And *vastu* encourages you to imitate nature in your approach to bringing beauty into the home. In her illuminating book *Vastu: Transcendental Home Design in Harmony with Nature* (Gibbs Smith), author Sherri Silverman describes the healing effect of beautiful objects or spaces, and in this sense the *vastu* approach to decorating a room is aimed at allowing it to function spiritually, through beauty, as well as physically. Silverman explains that *vastu* defines beauty in terms of *rasas*. A Sanskrit term, *rasa*

means "juice" or "sap," and represents the nuanced energetic essence of any kind of art or architecture that makes it pleasing, captures the imagination and leads to an experience described as *rasavadanda*, the sense of transcendence we experience in the face of true beauty, which communicates the hidden power behind the world by shining through a physical form.

Historically, the *vastu shastra upanishad* defines nine major *rasas*, or variations on the essence of beauty, including soothing or uplifting qualities such as tranquility, playfulness, heroism, wonder and romance, as well as darker sides of beauty such as fear, contemptuousness, anger and compassion. Choosing art and objects that embody the happier *rasas* will surely result in a more uplifting, inspiring home.

Color: Unlike *feng shui*'s clearly defined approach to using specific colors or groups of colors in the different *guas* of a home, *vastu* employs a more flexible method of integrating color into the home, which can be tailored to attune to the needs and inclinations of the individual. *Vastu*'s sister discipline *ayurveda* recognizes the healing

qualities of certain colors. Based on the colors of the rainbow, which correspond to the chakra system of subtle energy in the body developed by Indian mystics thousands of years ago, the ayurvedic approach to using colors involves choosing healing hues for a person based on his or her physical constitution.

The ayurvedic term for bodily constitution is *dosha*, and the discipline has defined three different *doshas*: *vata*, *pitta* and *kapha*, which exist to varying degrees in all people, yet for each individual one *dosha* tends to dominate. Each *dosha* consists of the interaction of the five elements—earth, air, water, fire and space. The ideal is to establish a balance among all three *doshas*. And among the many tools at their disposal to create this balance, ayurvedic healers use color to stimulate or soothe the tendencies that can be problematic for each *dosha* when out of balance.

Vata energy, which is a combination of the air and space elements, is sometimes referred to as the king of the *doshas*, as it moves before the others. *Vata* people tend to be slim and wiry with angular, often irregular features, and they often have dark hair. They are sensitive, artistic and imaginative, but can be anxious, excitable and nervous when under pressure. Elements in the home that can calm *vata* energy are plants and herbs with reassuring scents like lavender, juniper, rose, sage, cedarwood and camphor. Colors that help balance *vata* people are deep warm reds, which can give them the willpower to follow through on ideas, blue to help reduce insomnia, magenta to harmonize with other doshas, violet to calm the air and ether elements, and green to calm their propensity toward excess movement. Yellow is the one color that can aggravate *vata* people, leading to nervousness.

Pitta energy is associated with the element of fire, and is hot, explosive and can be transformative. *Pitta* people have medium builds, focused gazes, and are often fair-skinned. They are discriminating, confident and make good leaders, but they are also quick to anger. Elements in the home that can balance *pitta* energy are flowers and herbs with fresh, soothing aromas like gardenia, jasmine, lavender, lime and peppermint. Colors that balance excess *pitta* energy are turquoise, which cools the inflammation and fevers that are common to these types; indigo and blue, which are destressing; yellow, which brings objectivity; and magenta, which promotes a sense of peacefulness that can temper the ruthlessness that *pittas* can manifest when out of balance. Green is a balancing color for every *dosha*.

Kapha energy is composed of earth and water, and those with a dominant *kapha dosha* tend to be grounded and balanced, with oily skin, round faces and thick lustrous hair, full mouths and strong teeth. *Kapha* people are caring, compassionate, steady, reliable and forgiving. *Kapha* energy is situated in the chest area. Elements in the home that can balance *kapha* energy are plants and herbs that have a warming quality and stimulating scent, such as basil, bergamot, camphor, cinnamon, orange and peppermint. Good colors for *kapha* people are reds and oranges, which stimulate energy and vitality, as well as magenta, when you need to let go of old patterns and change. Green is also a good healing color that relates to the water element in *kapha* people.

Elements: Like *feng shui*, *vastu* aims to create spaces that enhance life by aligning a home with elements of nature. Each of the elements is associated with a particular direction, starting with the most ethereal or least dense—space or unmanifest energy—then evolving to the most dense or grossest.

• **Space:** This element, also known as ether, is linked with sound. It is positioned in the expansive center of the house or room, which should be kept open, free and clear of any obstructions to the flow of *prana*.

• **Air:** Like the wind, the air element represents movement, and the northwest area it's associated with is a good location for fans, chimes and air conditioners or purifiers. It's also a good place for windows.

• **Fire:** Associated with the southeast, fire in the body relates to digestion and the consumption of food and its subsequent conversion into fuel. As such, the southeast area of a home is the ideal location for a kitchen. The southeast area of any room is the best place for electrical equipment, such as computers, stereos and televisions.

• **Water:** The northeast area is associated with water, where its energies collect and bring healing qualities to a home. It is the best place for contemplative settings that include a fountain, pool or other fresh body of water.

• **Earth:** The heaviest element, earth grounds a home and is associated with the southwest corner of a home, the ideal location for a master bedroom. This area of the house should also include earth elements, such as plants, stones and trees.

mysticism

Jyotish (Vedic astrology): Another Vedic system that ancient sages used to reinforce the relationship of man to nature and the broader cosmos is called *jyotish*. A combination of astronomy and astrology, *jyotish* observes the effect of nine celestial bodies, known in Sanskrit as *grahas*, on our earth and our individual human natures. It also associates each planet with various colors and gemstones that reflect these colors. Each of the planets and their associated colors and stones correspond to *padas* in the *purusha mandala* that align with the cardinal and intermediate directions. The planets in the Vedic system are a little different than the planets in the solar system we can now see, thanks to advanced telescopes. They include the sun, moon, Mars, Mercury, Jupiter, Venus, Saturn, the north/ascending lunar node (*Rahu*), and the south/descending lunar node (*Ketu*).

The colors associated with the planets and the elements align for the most part with their physical qualities. Reds, oranges and yellows are good to use in the area of the sun, which is on the east side of a home. White, silver and gray are aligned with the northwest area of the moon. In the south, deep reds and oranges link with Mars, and in the north, Mercury is associated with green, which represents vibrancy and growth in the health and wealth sector of the *mandala*. Golden colors are appropriate for both Jupiter and Ketu in the northeast area, or gateway to the gods, yet blue hues can also be used to harmonize with the water element associated with this zone, while indigo and blues can soothe the planet Venus or cool the element of fire in the southeast. Apricot and gold also harmonize with the fire element in this area. In the west, *vastu* encourages deep colors like dark blue, black and violet, and in the southwest shades of golden brown or orange harmonize with the earth element.

Tools to rectify problem rooms or conditions: In addition to specific *yantras*, *vastu* practitioners use other means to rectify problem areas in a home, such as missing corners or extensions. Some use bricks, stones or wooden strips to create lines to complete the missing corner on the exterior of the house. Others use wind chimes, candles, water fountains, gemstones or other ornaments to honor the element or deity associated with the offended location.

What's Your Dominant Dosha?

Look at the list of qualities for each of the three *doshas* and give yourself 4 points for qualities that always apply, 2 for those that sometimes apply and 0 for those that never apply. Then add the numbers for each *dosha*. The one with the most points is your dominant *dosha*. If the scores of two *doshas* are close, you are bidoshic. If all three scores are almost the same, you're among the fortunate well-balanced tridoshic people.

Kapha qualities
• I have a solid build with big bones.
• I feel heavy after eating and my digestion is slow.
• I gain weight easily and have a hard time losing it.
• I am patient and even-tempered.
• I don't like humidity and dampness.
• I am considerate and caring.
• I am sometimes slow to grasp new concepts, but once I learn them I don't forget.

Pitta qualities
• I have a medium build and average weight.
• Sometimes I get a burning sensation with indigestion.
• I love iced drinks and cold foods.
• I am generally well-focused and alert.
• I can be impatient and get angry easily.
• I'm inspired by a challenge.
• I can be critical and stubborn.

Vata qualities
• I am slender and can eat whatever I want without gaining weight.
• I dislike cold weather, food and drinks.
• I have vivid dreams.
• I am creative and spirited.
• I get anxious and insecure when stressed.
• I like to travel.
• I learn new things easily but don't have great long-term memory.

How to Use a Purusha Mandala

Vastu practitioners use *purusha mandalas* to map the flow of *prana*, or cosmic energy, within a home or room. The *mandala* also aims to help you organize your home to best align with the forces of nature. Simply place the mandala over the floor plan of your home or room, aligning the north side of the *mandala* with the north side of your home to see whether your rooms fall into the most hospitable zones for their purpose. If changing a room or remodeling is neither practical nor affordable to you, consider applying some of the rectifications used by *vastu* practitioners to balance the energy.

Direction: Northwest
Vastu Element: Air
Colors: White, Silver and Gray
Gemstones: Pearl, Moonstone
Planet: Moon

According to *vastu*, the northwest area of the home is associated with the element of air, which represents movement. It's also associated with the moon, and so ethereal colors, like white, pale gray and silver, enhance this area of the home, which is ideal for guest rooms.

Direction: North
Life Area: Health and Wealth
Colors: Greens
Gemstones: Emerald, green tourmaline, jade, peridot
Planet: Mercury

If your finances feel blocked or your health is suffering, *vastu* suggests introducing green colors and elements, like art, gemstones, green wall paint and accents and even green plants, in the north side of your home to enhance health and wealth.

Direction: Northeast
Element: Water
Colors: Golden Yellows, Ochre or Yellow-Green
Life area: Spiritual Knowledge (gateway to the gods)
Gemstones: Citrine, Topaz
Planets: Jupiter, Ketu

The area of study, knowledge and meditation is the ideal place for quiet time and reflection and should be kept spotlessly clean.

Direction: West
Colors: Violet, Dark Blue and Black
Life area: The Unknown, Darkness
Gemstones: Blue Sapphire, Amethyst
Planet: Saturn

Associated with darkness and mystery and the setting sun, the western side of a *vastu* home is often the location of a stairway leading to another level. The deeper blues and dark colors associated with this part of a home are said to aid in fostering a sense of detachment.

Direction: Center
Element: Space

The center of a mandala represents the void from which all material forms and energy arise, and is associated with the space element. It is considered the heart and lungs of a home and should be left open and unobstructed to properly nourish the inhabitants.

Direction: East
Life area: Enlightenment and inspiration
Colors: Red, Orange, Yellow
Gemstones: Ruby, Garnet
Planet: Sun

The east side of the house and its association with the sun is enhanced with sunny colors like red, yellow and orange, which stimulate energy and encourage reception of the cosmic inspiration and enlightenment that is believed to emanate from the energy of the sun.

Direction: Southwest
Vastu Element: Earth
Colors: Orange, Golden brown or Red
Gemstones: Hessonite Garnet
Planet: Rahu

Associated with the earth element, the southwest area of a home is generally an ideal place for a master bedroom. Decorating it with earthy hues, such as warm browns, yellow and golds, will enhance the grounding vibrations associated with the location.

Direction: South
Colors: Deep Red, Orange and Coral
Life Area: Duty, Responsibility, Death
Gemstones: Oxblood, Red Coral
Planet: Mars

Red hues empower and stimulate the area of responsibility and duty in a *vastu* home. It's not necessary to paint the walls red if this hue is overpowering to you. Accents such as flowers, pillows or rugs will also suffice.

Direction: Southeast
Vastu Element: Fire
Colors: White, Indigo, Blue
Gemstones: Diamond, White Sapphire
Planet: Venus

Associated with the element of fire, the southeast side of a *vastu* house is a common place for the kitchen, where electrically powered appliances and gas-burning stoves are in their "element." Associated with Venus, this location is also sometimes used for bedrooms.

wabi-sabi

Unlike *feng shui* and *vastu*, which offer prescriptive approaches to living in harmony with nature, the Japanese art of *wabi-sabi* encourages making your home a sanctuary by tuning in to your own intuition. Instead of aiming to improve your living spaces by filling them with bigger, better and newer things, *wabi-sabi* encourages creating a richer life by cultivating a sense of appreciation for imperfection, impermanence and incompleteness.

The term *wabi-sabi* is difficult to translate into English. Various words have been used to define *wabi*, among them *tranquility, austerity, loneliness* and *quietude*. The origins of the word have been attributed to Japanese literature of the 5th and 6th centuries, when haiku poets used it to describe the loneliness of living in nature, remote from society. Some of the words used to define *sabi* are *age, leanness* and *rust*. Over time, the two words were joined to describe an aesthetic concept —linked in part to the tea ceremonies that emerged as important cultural rituals during the 16th and 17th centuries—and acquired more positive and hopeful connotations. *Wabi*, in this merged context, has been translated to mean "rustic simplicity," "humble by choice" and "harmony with nature." *Sabi* refers to the beauty that comes with the character, grace and patina of age. Together, the words have been translated to mean "wisdom in simple beauty" or "flawed beauty."

Wabi-sabi also carries a spiritual component that is intimately tied to Zen Buddhism, which regards the understanding of emptiness and imperfection as an essential first step to *satori*, or enlightenment. *Wabi-sabi* nurtures a sense of authenticity and truth by embracing and accepting the ideas that nothing is perfect, everything changes and nothing lasts indefinitely. And these ideas are practiced and expressed in Japanese arts and crafts as well as in everyday activities. By turning our attention toward finding beauty in what seems ordinary—falling leaves, for example, or cracks in rustic pottery—we become more deeply engaged in life and more conscious of the natural, changing, unique objects around us, which helps us to connect more profoundly to the real world and avoid stressful or meaningless distractions.

beyond style

Although rusting metal, aged wood and faded fabric are important parts of the *wabi-sabi* aesthetic, it is more than a look or style that you can introduce to your home. *Wabi-sabi* is an attitude, a way of living that encourages you to slow down in this materialistic, techonology-saturated world and take the time to enjoy simple pleasures, such as crafting a handmade gift for a family member or making and sharing a cup of tea with a friend.

Indeed, in Japan, the tea ceremony, as well as all of the accoutrements, rituals and structures that go along with it, has become emblematic of the *wabi-sabi* ideal. Initially the preserve of 12th-century ascetic monks, the practice of tea took root on a broader scale over the centuries, and other arts—from poetry and architecture to flowers and cuisine—evolved around it, entrenching the aesthetic in the wider culture. In her book *The Wabi-Sabi House* (Clarkson Potter), author Robyn Griggs Lawrence explains that manners and behavior are as important to the *wabi-sabi* point of view as objects and ideas. The quiet, gracious tea ceremony also spawned an etiquette associated with the practice that embodies four principles of *wabi-sabi*—harmony, respect, purity and tranquility. And the *wabi-sabi* aesthete brings these ideas beyond the confines of the tearoom into every aspect of daily life. "The intangibles, the small daily acts that have nothing to do with decorating, organizing your living space or embracing im-

Wabi-Sabi

Asymmetry: From gardens to interiors, the aesthetic generally follows the unwritten rule of uneven numbers in furnishings and accents.

Restraint: *Shibui*, the Japanese art of "not too much" or the "cultivation of little," is integral to a *wabi-sabi* home and celebrates a sense of unassuming humility and quietness.

Modesty: Humble, handcrafted objects are honored.

Intimacy: Whether you're communing with nature or an honored guest, *wabi-sabi* celebrates a sense of quiet respect in all interactions.

Utility: If something isn't useful, it isn't beautiful to the *wabi-sabi* aesthete.

Naturalness: Natural elements such as wood bring a sense of authenticity and unpretentiousness to *wabi-sabi* rooms.

Not Wabi-Sabi

Mass production: Mass-produced technology, appliances and machine-made utensils and objects oppose the imperfection and handicraft embraced by *wabi-sabi* aesthetes.

Finery: Lace, porcelain and other trappings of a materialistic lifestyle have no place in a *wabi-sabi* room.

Competition: The *wabi-sabi* person practices a sense of nonjudgmental detachment from worldly pursuits and cultivates a sense of being satisfied with life as it is.

Noise: The sounds of nature agree with the spirit of *wabi-sabi;* revving machines and amplified music do not. The same holds true for the visual noise of clutter.

perfection…are the *wabi-sabi* lessons that can make a home happier and more peaceful," says Griggs-Lawrence.

cleanliness and order

Given *wabi-sabi*'s embrace of imperfection, it would be tempting to use it as an excuse for allowing dirt and disorder to creep into your rooms. But slovenliness is not what *wabi-sabi* is about. In fact, clutter and grime are antithetical to the essence of the aesthetic. *Wabi-sabi* is about paring back your belongings and choosing to live only with things you love, need and respect—worn and weathered though they may be. In describing the evolution of this approach to living, the renowned architect Tadao Ando says, "The Japanese view of life embraced a simple aesthetic that grew stronger as inessentials were eliminated and trimmed away." In stripping away the superfluous, a kind of quiet romance with what is genuinely meaningful begins.

cycles and seasons

Paying attention to seasonal changes reminds us that we, like the leaves on a tree, are part of a natural order. And in the *wabi-sabi* aesthete's vigilant mindfulness of what is happening in the here and now, he is attuned to the changes in the natural world around him and is also at peace with the natural cycle of growth, decay and death. This mindset aligns with a Buddhist concept known as *annica*, or the law of impermanence. By celebrating every stage in this cycle, we tap into part of the spiritual essence of the *wabi-sabi*—and experience the serenity that springs from it.

To make this idea manifest at home, Griggs Lawrence suggests choosing objects that "resonate with the spirit of their makers' hands and hearts: the chair your grandfather made, your six-year-old's lumpy pottery, an afghan you knitted yourself (out of handspun sheep's wool, perhaps)." She also notes that the colors in a *wabi-sabi* room tend to be muted—gray, slate, brown, black—while materials are natural and prone to weathering, lending an air of perishability.

Another way to embrace and celebrate the change that comes with the seasons is to bring elements of nature into your home and adapt your surroundings to accommodate the unique qualities that seasonal elements contribute to your space. Branches of intense yellow forsythia or bunches of bright pink tulips in spring practically beg you to roll up the woolly carpets and switch out the velvet pillows that so ably warmed the house in winter, while the fragile fading leaves and exposed branches of autumn quietly insist that you make the transition from summer's exuberant hues and the outdoors toward quieter colors and interior comforts, like handmade quilts, teapots, knit throws, candles and chenille cushions, which signal a phase of turning inward.

science & poetics

While *vastu* experts and *feng shui* masters rely on constitutional or astrological analyses to get a picture of who people are and what their personality is like before making recommendations on how to shape living spaces to accommodate them, Western social scientists, industrial psychologists and environmental behavioral psychologists have other ways of assessing personality types and the impact of the environment on the human psyche based on their own body of research. Furniture manufacturers, industrial engineers, designers and architects have relied on this research to create products and commercial buildings that support optimal human activity and responses. But in the home, much of this research has gone untapped.

the psyche of home

Although various American architects—including Frank Lloyd Wright and Bernard Maybeck in the early 20th century and Robert A.M. Stern and Jeremiah Eck in the 21st century—have made it their mission to create houses that attune to both the environmental context as well as subtle human needs, many of today's spec builder houses lack the sense of comfort and excitement that would bring out the best in the people who live in them. In her book *House Thinking* (HarperCollins), author Winifred Gallagher examines much of this available yet underused environmental behavioral research, including recent efforts undertaken by architect, scholar and teacher Grant Hildebrand along with colleagues at the University of Washington, which uncovered five universal qualities in residential dwellings that elicit innate positive human responses. The team defined these qualities as: prospect, refuge, enticement, peril and complex order. Architects like Wright and Maybeck intuitively incorporated these ideas into their designs. But by pinpointing these qualities and clearly defining them, the research team provides insight into how any home can be built to elicit positive emotional and behavioral responses in addition to being aesthetically appealing and functional.

To understand the notions of "prospect" and "refuge," explains Gallagher, it is helpful to think of them together on opposite ends of a continuum, with refuge exemplifying the sense of comfort that comes from cozy, contained sheltering spaces and elements, such as inglenooks, window seats and fireplaces, and prospect representing areas or elements that open up a home to the wider world and views of nature beyond, such as balconies, decks and picture windows. When both of these qualities are built into a home, says the author, a dwelling, in effect, becomes "a womb with a view."

"Enticement," from an architectural point of view, is the element of surprise afforded by a peek into a space beyond an entrance hall,

a sheltered passage or a winding path that invites investigation to find the promise of a haven or intriguing view around the bend. An interest in "peril" in the home may seem counterintuitive, but when viewed from within a safe haven, perilous scenes, such as an untamed wilderness or a dramatic storm, become wondrous and exciting rather than alarming. Finally, the researchers attribute the appeal of "complex order" to the sophisticated human brain, which evolved and is wired to absorb and process volumes of data and ideas and sort them into highly developed categories. And this innate human ability explains our attraction to houses with an array of distinctly configured rooms dedicated to different purposes, defined with different materials, and outfitted with different forms of seating, tables, chairs, pillows, books and objects. These layers of complexity create an ambience of sensory stimulation and fascination that bland, boxy homogeneous spaces can in fact undermine.

Assigning specific roles to different rooms doesn't just stimulate our complex brains. Giving rooms distinct purposes also subliminally enables an individual to experience the nuances of his or her psyche on different levels, allowing one's different personae to unfold from room to room. A welcoming entrance, for example, can help a woman shift from manager to mom at the end of a day, or comfortable bedding and soft lighting in a bedroom can let a man go from father to lover within the confines of one domain.

Yet the specific qualities of a house that enable these psychological shifts vary from person to person. If you want to create a comfortable, nurturing environment that positively impacts you from a behavioral perspective, Gallagher suggests trying to identify aspects of homes you loved and hated in the past, rather than bringing home paint chips or clipping images from magazines. Recalling colors of rooms that elicit happy memories, or that gave you the creeps, for that matter, can help you shape rooms that bring out your best. The same holds true for architectural elements, such as doorknobs, paneling or bookshelves, or objects, such as a table made by a grandfather or vase once owned by a favorite aunt.

home as archetype

Everything about a house—from its size, scale and proportions to its architectural style and the character of its rooms—resonates on different levels for different people. Yet, according to Gallagher, some environmental research shows that various types of houses tend to elicit common responses in most Americans, which helps to clarify our cultural associations with certain historical residential structures. Brick houses, for example, generally convey a sense of higher status, while farmhouses are seen as friendly, and Tudors and Colonials represent prestige.

On the other hand, studies on the evolution of different rooms in the house show parallels in social change, revealing how advancements in the home affect our psyches and reflect shifts in collective attitudes. A recent exhibition called "Counter Space: Design and the Modern Kitchen" at the Museum of Modern Art in New York City, for example, chronicled the evolution of the kitchen over the past century from a dirty, harsh, closed-off space often banished or disengaged from the living areas of the home to an open hub of activity and heart of the home. It also illustrated the link between its gradual yet dramatic transformation and the improved status of women. Similarly, an exploration of research on the history of the bathroom—including the fact that its current place inside the home is a relatively recent historical development—can reveal much about our ever-evolving collective view of sewage and hygiene, as well as beauty, self-esteem and comfort.

physiology and the home

Other research focuses on the impact of our environment on our physiology, which in turn affects our psychological state. Many have heard about research that links a lack of sunlight, especially during the winter months, to a condition known as seasonal affective disorder (SAD), or the winter blues, whose symptoms include lack of energy, moodiness or even depression. But research linking productivity to nature's diurnal rhythms is less well known. Thanks to this research, however, designers of office spaces now consistently design work environments to allow everyone to have access to light and views, which help regulate our bodily rhythms and give us the energy and sense of well-being we need to get productively and healthily through a day. Having access to sunlight and being able to chart the arc of the sun through the sky over the course of the day is equally important in our homes, allowing our internal clocks to quietly wind down as the sun begins to set and prepare us for a healthy night's sleep.

Other research has supported the concept of universal design, which grew out of the Americans with Disabilities Act and aims to cre-

Organizing for Your Personality Type

Everyone's idea of order is unique. Some people like to create pristine stacks, and others have an innate urge to spread out their stuff where they can see it. These differences can be attributed to how our brains are wired. In general, people are either left-brained or right-brained, and these two types have contrasting ways of seeing and categorizing the world around them. If you pay attention to your personality type it can be easier to come up with organizing systems that complement your nature. Here are some tips on how to organize for each type.

Left-brained people prefer designated locations for everything and like to sort. Storage options with compartments are ideal for these types, who generally like to keep their stuff out of sight, too. Stacking boxes with lids are also helpful for left-brainers, as are files with tabs or labels that help them organize by date or object type. Left-brainers also like to sort clothes by type and color and hang them on matching hangers for a neat, consistent appearance.

Right-brained people have trouble adhering to strict schemes and can benefit from creative, emotionally inspiring storage solutions. Think garden urns as magazine files, or buckets as garden-tool totes. If you find there's at least some method to your organizing madness, dropping a bag on a chair in the entrance hall, for example, or leaving jewelry on your bedside table, you might consider placing a tray on the night table for jewelry or putting a coat tree near the entrance for bags and jackets.

ate spaces that allow a universal sense of ease in built spaces, whether a person is fully functional or disabled, has vision or is blind, is short or tall, young or old. Some of the kinds of adaptations made to standard design to allow for universal access are high-contrast surfaces that promote visibility, countertops at varying heights to allow access whether standing or seated, ample shower stalls with places to sit or stand, and door handles with levers rather than knobs that are easy to move up and down whether your fingers are nimble or not.

a poetic view of home

Even the nooks and crannies of a house, and its nether reaches, leave their imprint on the deeper recesses of our psyches—for good or for bad. In his iconic book *The Poetics of Space* (Beacon Press), the philosopher Gaston Bachelard offers a lyrical exploration of the home—from cellar to attic—and through it shows how our perceptions and impressions of our shelters conspire to shape our memories, thoughts and dreams. "Our house is our corner of the world…

our first universe, a real cosmos in every sense of the word," he says. "If we look at it intimately, the humblest dwelling has beauty…. An entire past comes to dwell in a new house. And the daydream deepens to the point where an immemorial domain opens up for the dreamer." By reflecting on our childhood homes and tuning into the feelings they evoke, he argues, we can bring those memories and fantasies to every susbsequent home we occupy and thereby shape them in to nests for dreaming and shelters for the imagination, places where we can connect with the most intimate aspects of our natures.

Mark Twain, one of America's most famous writers and literary icons, attributed a special kind of energy to his own home, which he believed nourished him and his family with happiness and support during the years when he wrote *The Adventures of Tom Sawyer, Huckleberry Finn* and *The Prince and the Pauper,* among other of his most famous works. In a letter he wrote to a friend, he offers a wonderfully evocative interpretation of the spirit of this home: "To us our house was not unsentient matter—it had a heart and a soul and eyes to see us with; and approvals, and solicitudes, and deep sympathies; it was of us, and we were in its confidence, and lived in its grace and in the peace of its benediction. We never came home from an absence that its face did not light up and speak out its eloquent welcome—and we could not enter it unmoved."

In contrast, poet laureate Dr. Maya Angelou shares a personal account of a darker side of the spirit of a house in her autobiographical essay "A House Can Hurt, a Home Can Heal." Describing the home she shared with her husband at the time, she writes, "The living room was two stories high, and I put my three-by-five-foot paintings on the walls, and upon those vast reaches they diminished and began to look little better than enlarged color posters. I laid my Indian and Pakistani rugs on the floor over the beige wall-to-wall carpeting and they drowned in the vastness of the living room, appearing little more than colorful table mats on a large boardroom table. Everything was built-in—standard oven, microwave oven, grill, garbage disposal, compactor. There was nothing for my husband to do." This house, she believes, was responsible for the start of a separation between herself and her husband, and the next house they purchased together, though more charming on the surface, completed the split. "My drapes, hung by professionals, came off the runners. The doors began not to fit the frame, and my piano would not stay in tune. The house hated us," she writes of this second house.

After parting with her spouse and moving to North Carolina, however, she found a house that aligned with her spirit in a positive way. "I bought the house, and as I refurbished it, it also molded me. I

Sweet Dreams

Getting a good night's sleep year-round is essential to living a healthy and wholesome life. In a survey on American sleep habits, the Better Sleep Council learned that 65 percent of Americans are losing sleep due to stress and that 32 percent lose sleep at least one night a week. To ensure you get restorative sleep, consider these tips from the Council:

- **Make sleep a priority** by keeping a consistent bedtime and waking schedule, including on weekends.
- **Create a bedtime routine that is relaxing.** Experts recommend reading a book, listening to soothing music or soaking in a hot bath.
- **Transform your bedroom into a haven of comfort.** Create a room that is dark, quiet, comfortable and cool for the best possible sleep.
- **Evaluate your mattress and pillow to ensure proper comfort and support.** If your mattress is five to seven years old, it may be time for a new one. In general, pillows should be replaced every year.
- **Keep work materials, computers and televisions out of the bedroom;** it should be used for sleep and sex only.
- **Exercise regularly,** but complete your workout at least two hours before bedtime.
- **If you sleep with a partner, your mattress should allow each of you enough space to move easily.** Couples who have been sleeping on a "double" (full size) may think they have enough room, until they learn that each person has only as much sleeping space as a baby's crib!
- **Avoid using nicotine, caffeine and alcohol close to bedtime.** They can lead to poor sleep.
- **Finish eating** at least two to three hours before bedtime.

added a bedroom for my grandson, who had been missing for four years. He was returned as the room was completed. A man whom I had adored from a distance declared his undying love for me. When I took the house it had ten rooms, and I have added on more…. This is no longer my house," she writes, "it is my home."

If we take the time to explore our most intimate associations with home, as many talented architects, scientists, philosophers and poets have done and urge us to do, then we may be able to more consciously and effectively shape our spaces in ways that can help us not only to overcome emotional issues from the past, but also to reignite our fondest memories, stoke our imaginations and positively synthesize our shelters with our souls.

substance

If the spirit of a home is about the intangibles that enhance its comfort, the substance of a home is about the material things that enrich its value. While there are signs that the housing market in this country is beginning to stabilize, the turnaround is expected to be gradual, so many Americans have committed to staying in their existing homes and renovating them to increase their value and improve quality of life, rather than moving out to move up. There are myriad ways to add value to your home.

Coffered ceilings and recessed lighting add character and comfort to this renovated home near Washington, DC. Shutters on the windows are an easy-care window treatment option for busy parents with four children.

You can make it safer or more energy-efficient, improve the efficiency of its layout, update a kitchen or bath, create usable space in a basement or attic, and improve outdoor living spaces, to name a few. Yet these kinds of upgrades can require a fairly substantial outlay of cash. If your budget is limited but your willingness to invest some sweat equity is great, you can also make modest home improvements that will increase the value of your home and improve the quality of your life without necessarily spending a bundle. Some of these efforts include refacing or repainting kitchen cabinets, replacing kitchen counters, adding molding and trim, painting walls, replacing or refinishing wood floors, improving your landscape and adding built-in storage, among many other less costly yet significant upgrades.

building and renovating

If you're planning a renovation, consider not just the capital improvement value the effort will add to your home, but the utility value, too. The latter is a term used by real estate professionals to describe the value an improvement brings to your home by enhancing the quality of your life while you continue to live in it. Only you can really determine what this value is. The capital improvement value, on the other hand, is easier to measure in terms what you'll get back for the money you put in, as experts regularly track changes in the percentage of returns on investments for home improvements.

investing wisely

Since the housing crisis unfolded in 2008, a number of shifts have occurred in the kinds of renovations that have been taking place nationwide. According to a study by the Joint Center for Housing Studies of Harvard University, prior to the housing collapse, when house prices were on the rise over the previous several decades, Americans tended to invest in discretionary home improvements, such as kitchen and bath renovations, as a wealth-building strategy. Now with house prices depressed, owners are more likely to make improvements that maintain the structural integrity and efficient functioning of their homes, as well as those that generate cost savings. This type of remodeling effort includes window replacement or electrical, plumbing and HVAC upgrades, for example, and is expected to continue into the years ahead, particularly as these kinds of upgrades can save you money over the long haul with reduced energy costs. But as the economy begins to turn around, and people begin to buy new and existing homes again, discretionary interior improvements are likely to gradually pick up, too.

cost vs. value

Prior to the housing collapse, it was common to recoup 100 percent or more of certain remodeling investments, such as a kitchen renovation, for example. Nowadays, the return on investments has dropped, but you can still recover a substantial portion of your investment on numerous upgrades—and remember to factor in the utility value you'll reap from the improvement while you live in the home, too. Among the projects offering the highest return on investment, according to the Hanley Wood Cost vs. Value Report, a reliable industry index, converting an attic into a bedroom will yield an average 83 percent return. Other projects that offer substantial returns are steel entry door replacements, wood deck additions, basement remodels, minor kitchen remodels, vinyl siding replacement and window replacement, all of which recoup 75 percent or more of your investment. Major kitchen and bath remodels also offer substantial returns of more than 71 percent of costs.

planning & budgeting

It's been said that a good home is never done. We all make gradual changes to our home to adapt to our needs as we grow, and we repair or replace aging materials, appliances and furnishings as they fade out. But sometimes a room or a whole house needs a total makeover. And when that time comes, it's helpful to map out a game plan and establish a budget and timeframe so that you'll be in charge of the outcome. Whether you're refurnishing a living room, converting an attic into a bedroom, or remodeling a kitchen or bath, start by establishing a clear budget and completion date and work backward to devise a game plan for your goals. The next step is to shop around and compare prices for products and labor to see if your dreams are in line with your budget. Prices for a sofa can range from less than $1,000 to more than $20,000; a sink from $100 to $3,500. A complete kitchen renovation is one of the costliest home improvement efforts you can make. But the range in price for a complete kitchen redo is extreme—starting at around $20,000 for a modest makeover in a small town and running up to $100,000 or more for a spectacular kitchen remodel with luxurious materials and top-of-the-line appliances in a large suburban home.

If, after making a reality check, you find your budget doesn't align with your dreams, you can start making decisions about trade-offs. For example, you can buy a couple of gallons of paint, a roller, brushes and a paint pan, and repaint a small room yourself for under $100. Or you can pay someone else to do it for between $250 to $1,000 a room, not including supplies. You can get a 1,500-square-foot wood floor buffed and recoated for around $3,000, or you can buy a new

Pulling Permits

If a contractor asks you to pull your own permits, the National Association of the Remodeling Industry (NARI) advises looking for a different one. Relying on a contractor to navigate the permitting process can save you time, money and stress. It's part of the service that a consumer should expect when hiring a contractor.

Cities use permits to regulate construction and help ensure that it is safe. A permit is an agreement that whatever work is being done to a home complies with your area's building codes. Most government bodies adopt codes for construction, mechanical, plumbing and electrical features. In addition, there are federal, state and local laws that govern construction, such as those covering energy conservation. For more information on the National Association of the Remodeling Industry or to find a contractor in your area, visit its site at *nari.org*. For green remodeling information, visit *greenremodeling.org*.

Ways to Save

To add value to your home, consider these options:

• **Search online for pricing** of exactly the same product as well as similar products.
• **Avoid moving plumbing or electrical unless necessary,** and try to work within an existing footprint if possible.
• **Purchase several appliances from the same venue** and ask for a discount. You're more likely to get one when you purchase a group of products at once.
• **Ask your designer** to specify standard sizes for cabinets, pullouts and doors whenever possible to avoid upcharges for special requests or unusual custom features.
• **Search websites,** such as *eBay.com, Craigslist.org* or *DiggersList.com* for used or surplus materials or products at discounted prices.

one for around $20,000. According to the National Kitchen & Bath Association, for kitchen projects, cabinets and hardware will usually account for about 29 percent of your investment, appliances and ventilation about 14 percent, countertops about 10 percent and installation about 17 percent. For a bath, more than half your budget will go toward fixtures, cabinets and installation. The faucets and plumbing in a bath can account for about 14 percent of your budget. The cost of labor for demolition, plumbing, electricity, tiling and other building trade work varies widely from region to region.

For more information on remodeling a kitchen or bath, including advice on budgeting and controlling costs, visit the National Kitchen & Bath Association's website at *nkba.org/tips*.

finding a contractor

With increased competition in the remodeling industry, many contractors are now emphasizing project pricing (rather than their credentials, customer satisfaction record or breadth of services) as their principal advantage. A recent poll conducted by Angie's List, an online

Home Economics

You don't have to have a fortune to enhance your home. Consider the following ways to add value to your home at different price points. If you have:

$50–100

- Paint a room in a neutral color.
- Hire a designer for an hour to offer ideas on simple improvements, such as new light fixtures or a more efficient furniture arrangement.
- Enlist an inspector to look at your basement, crawl spaces and attic and check for dry rot in the flooring joists or for gas or air leaks that should be repaired or sealed.

$100–$500

- Get a popcorn ceiling refinished.
- Hire a landscaper or lawn service to clean your gutters, clip overgrown bushes and prune your trees.
- Hire a cleaning service to deep clean your home, including baseboards and grout.
- Install a ceiling fan to freshen your house and provide energy savings.
- Install a water filtration system.

$500–$1,000

- Trade in an old water heater for a new tankless version, which heats water only when you need it and will save money on your energy bill.
- Replace an old appliance with a new Energy Star–qualified model, which may use 10 to 50 percent less energy or water and cut utility bills substantially.
- Update the floor tile in the bathroom for the biggest return on investment.
- Clear out a jammed wardrobe closet by removing half the clothes, then maximize the vertical real estate by installing a custom closet insert.

- Get ready-made or custom slipcovers for a sofa and/or chairs.

$1,000–$2,000

- Have crown molding around the ceiling installed by a pro.
- Get a new front door.
- Get a whole-house fan. It's less expensive than air conditioning, and especially if you have a vaulted ceiling, will save you money on electricity.
- Reupholster some chairs or buy a new sofa.

$2,000–$3,000

- Replace a laminate countertop in a kitchen with one made of stone or engineered stone.
- Expand your view by installing a larger window or sliding glass door.
- Upgrade appliances in the kitchen or a faucet and sink in the bath.

$3,000–$5,000

- Refinish a wood floor.
- Install or upgrade a storage system in your garage.
- Replace worn carpet or install an engineered wood floor in one room.
- Resurface a concrete driveway or patio that's been cracked or damaged by tree roots or the elements.

$5,000+

- Paint exterior siding.
- Add solar panels to supplement your electricity.
- Convert an unfinished basement or attic into usable space.
- Undertake a minor kitchen remodel, such as replacing countertops and appliances, and painting cabinets or getting new doors.

contractor referral service, found that 76 percent of contractors said that, in the current market, they would consider dropping their prices to get a project. Of these, 70 percent were willing to cut prices up to 10 percent; 25 percent were willing to cut prices 10 to 20 percent; and 5 percent were willing to offer even steeper discounts. The best way to find a contractor is through a referral by someone you know and trust. Another option is to use a number of online referral services, which don't guarantee a satisfactory outcome but can supply you with a list of firms in your area that you can contact and vet yourself. Among the online services available are Angie's List, DiggersList, ServiceMagic and CertaPro, though there are several others.

If you find a contractor through a website, be sure to request references and ask if you can stop by a site he's working on or see photographs of completed work. Also, check with your state's contractors licensing board to see if any complaints have been filed on him. Another option is to visit the site of the National Association of the Remodeling Industry (NARI), which can provide you with a referral. Be sure to interview at least three firms about your project and get estimates from each, which they'll generally offer for free.

Paperwork

If you live in a multi-unit dwelling like I do, anytime you make substantial building changes, you'll need to go through the requisite

Top 10 Upgrades That Add Value

1. Maintain your home. Buyers want homes in move-in condition with good floors, counters and cabinets. Appraisers say the best cosmetic investment is in neutral paint and new carpet—if you spend $1,500 to $3,500 on these things, it could be worth $5,000 to the buyer. Freshen-up projects, such as installing crown moldings and larger baseboards, will add value.

2. Install a new entry door. This will add the most value and may be the least costly improvement you can make. Spending an average of $1,200 for a new steel door, for example, should yield $1,500 in resale value, enabling you to recoup about 129 percent of your cost.

3. Replace siding. For upscale projects, fiber-cement siding replacement offers the highest percentage of cost recouped.

On an investment of about $13,000, you can get a resale value of about 84 percent.

4. Create an attic bedroom. This project has become more popular recently because of cost recouped. Although an average price tag for this kind of project is about $50,000, it's one of the most affordable ways to add conditioned living space to your home, yielding about 83 percent of its cost in resale value. Because you've already got the roof, joists and walls, taking advantage of costs that have already been covered, this kind of project makes sense.

5. Add a wood deck. This will increase your home's curb appeal and improve your quality of life. On average, in this market, a new $10,000 wood deck will return almost 81 percent of its cost.

6. Undertake a minor kitchen upgrade. A minor kitchen remodel will recoup an average of 78 percent of cost. This remodel

includes replacing cabinet fronts, the oven and the cooktop, and installing new laminate counters, resilient flooring, a new sink and faucet. Replacing old appliances with efficient Energy Star–rated appliances also saves money on energy bills long-term. An average minor kitchen remodel cost is about $24,000. The average price for a midrange kitchen remodel in America is about $57,000. A major remodel will return 72 percent of your investment.

7. Replace windows with energy-efficient versions. Upgrades that add to curb appeal will always have higher returns. Energy-efficient dual- and triple-paned windows save money on energy bills over the long haul, too, by as much as 15 to 20 percent. And tax credits, available through 2016 through the American Recovery and Reinvestment Act for qualified window components, boost the payback.

8. Remodel the basement. Turning unfinished basement space into usable areas with a television room and bar, for example, will return an average of 76 percent of your investment. Creating a walkout basement is even better.

9. Minor bath remodels can also yield a substantial return on investment. In baths with old tile and fixtures, if you spend $1,200 on a new shower or $500 for a new tile floor, some appraisers think you could get up to an 80 percent return. Even if you don't replace the tile, but re-grout, seal and caulk it, you can a good payback. A midrange bathroom remodel may cost an average of around $16,000; an upscale bathroom remodel may cost upward of $53,000.

10. Expand your space. Adding on a family room, garage or master suite can recoup 65 percent of costs. Appraisers say that in this market, three-bedroom homes are preferred over two-bedroom ones.

---

paperwork with your building management. If you live in a house or townhouse, you'll need to work with your local building department. You may need all of the subcontractors to sign off on an alteration agreement and supply certificates of insurance, which include workers' compensation and a minimum level of liability (though this is negotiable in some cases). You may also need to supply the subcontractors with certificate of capital improvement forms, which they keep in their files so that you won't have to pay sales tax on portions of your upgrades. If you work with a general contractor, you'll be spared much of this paperwork, as the contractor will serve as the clearinghouse for these matters. According to the National Association of the Remodeling Industry, your contractor should also be responsible for pulling all the necessary permits required to do the job.

Once you settle on your contractor, you'll need to clearly define the scope of work to avoid any surprise charges along the way. A common practice among contractors these days is to bid low to get the job and then accrue charges for unanticipated efforts along the way to inflate the final bill. The more clearly you define your initial scope of work from the start, the more likely you are to avoid this kind of situation. For once the work is done, a contractor can put a lien on your property for any charges you dispute. And if upheld, this lien will be recorded on your deed, making your home difficult to sell until it is cleared.

Before starting your project, establish your budget and build in at least a 10 to 20 percent cushion to cover extra costs that are bound to occur, including delivery charges, overruns, tips and extra materials, among other things. (Once work begins, create a punch list that can help guide the completion of tasks large and small as you go along.) Before starting a job, get a written estimate with detailed specifications on all the products and services, and work out a timetable for payment to your contractor or installer. Many ask for 35 to 50 percent up front, 35 percent when the job is substantially complete and the balance on completion.

If a designer is involved, you may pay a design fee, which will generally amount to about 4 percent of your total budget. Alternatively, you may be asked to pay a retainer. Whatever the charges may be, never pay 100 percent up front. And always ask what kind of warranties or guarantees a contractor or installer might offer on workmanship or product, and request to see a license, insurance and any other required documents before committing.

Tip: Among the valuable rules of thumb I gathered in the course of planning for my own home improvements was a tip I received from the real estate developer and A&E television host Armando Montelongo. He told me that if you want to get a decent return on your home improvement investment, you should invest no more than 10 to 15 percent of the current value of your home.

enhancing energy efficiency

Among the most popular remodeling efforts undertaken these days are improvements that can enhance the energy efficiency of your home. In the United States, electrical power is generated by facilities that rely on coal mostly, natural gas, or nuclear power—all sources that come with serious environmental caveats. As for usage and price (the dollar amount varies by region—from about 5 to 16 ¢ per kilowatt-hour), the average American household uses about 11,000 kilowatt-hours per year at an average annual residential electrical price tag of around $1,000. Here are some of the things you can do to conserve energy in your home.

• **Update appliances:** If you're in the market for a new appliance, remember to factor in the cost of owning it as well as the price of the appliance itself. A low-cost appliance could wind up costing you more over the long haul on the cost of repairs and maintenance as well as the cost to operate it.

How do you determine how much an appliance's energy consumption can affect your out-of-pocket costs? Let's say you're looking to buy a new refrigerator-freezer. Different models of refrigerators with the same capacity can vary dramatically in the amount of electricity they use—from a low of about 600 kilowatt-hours a year to a high of more than 800 kilowatt-hours a year. This means the annual cost to operate a refrigerator of this size can range from about $50 to $70, depending on which model you buy. A $20 difference in annual operating costs might not sound like much, but keep in mind that you will reap these savings for the life of the appliance.

You can learn about the energy efficiency of any appliance that you're thinking about buying through the yellow and black Energy Guide label it must display to meet the Federal Trade Commission's Appliance Labeling Rule. The law requires that the labels specify the capacity of the particular model, its estimated annual energy consumption and the range of estimated annual energy consumption of comparable appliances.

• **Replace windows and doors:** Another common upgrade to enhance energy efficiency these days is the replacement of old inefficient windows and doors. Very old single-pane windows are the biggest energy wasters, as they provide virtually no insulation from the outside air, but even older double-pane windows can be problematic. Installing Energy Star–qualified windows, doors and skylights can shrink energy bills by about 7 to 15 percent over nonqualified products, saving you between $146 and $501 per year depending on the heating and cooling costs in your region. You should always choose windows that are

Cash for Appliances

Many states are now offering rebate programs approved by the U.S. Department of Energy for the purchase of new Energy Star–qualified appliances. Most rebate amounts range from $50 to $500, depending upon the product, the purchase price and other market factors. Consumers may also be able to combine the state rebate with a local utility rebate, but eligibility should be verified with both organizations. Visit *energysavers.gov/financial/70022.html* to find out about your state's appliance rebate program and download rebate forms.

Tip: According to Dave Burcher, the New York–based kitchen designer who designed my kitchen, stainless-steel appliances remain the preferred choice for new and remodeled kitchens today, despite their propensity to show fingerprints and streaks. His secret to keeping stainless-steel appliances clean? Mix equal parts water and alcohol in a spray bottle, spray it over the surface of the appliance, then wipe it clean with a microfiber cloth. Follow with a coat of 3M's spray-on Stainless Steel Cleaner and Polish, wiping over the surface with another microfiber cloth. It works like a charm.

appropriate for the climate conditions in your area. The Energy Star website (*energystar.gov*) offers information that can guide your choices.

• **Seal and insulate:** One the most cost-effective ways to improve the energy efficiency and comfort of a home is to seal and insulate its envelope—the outer walls, ceiling, windows, doors and floors. Doing so can save up to 20 percent on your heating and cooling costs—or up to 10 percent on your total energy bill.

Many air leaks and drafts are easy to find because you can easily feel them around windows and doors. But holes that aren't easy to feel—in attics, basements and crawlspaces—are more problematic. Sealing these leaks with caulk, spray foam or weatherstripping can dramatically improve your comfort and reduce utility bills. Test for gaps around windows and doors by dampening your hand and running it around the edges, noting the areas that feel cooler. Seal the gaps with latex window caulk or foam sealant. Seal door bottoms with stick-on weatherstripping, which you can get for $5 to $10 at a home improvement or hardware store. Doing so can save you between $100 and $300 on your winter heating bill.

In houses with forced-air heating and cooling systems, ducts distribute conditioned air throughout the house. But in the average house, about 20 percent of the air that moves through the system is lost due to leaks, resulting in higher utility bills. Because some ducts are concealed in walls and between floors, repairing them can be difficult. But you can repair exposed ducts in attics, basements, crawlspaces and garages yourself by sealing the leaks with duct sealant.

If you're not using your fireplace, block it off to keep warm air from escaping. You can purchase a fireplace seal at a home store or block it off with cardboard or an expanding foam, such as Dap Kwik Foam, found at hardware stores.

Insulation keeps your home warm in winter and cool in summer. When correctly installed with air sealing, each type of insulation can deliver comfort and lower energy bills during the hottest and coldest times of the year. To get the biggest savings, add insulation in the attic. If your insulation is level with or below the attic floor joists, you probably need to add more. Also, be sure to choose the right kind of insulation for your climate type.

Another place to add insulation is around the ducts of a forced-air heating system that run through the unheated parts of your house, like the garage and attic. Measure the ducts in these areas and purchase precut insulation, which costs about $1 per linear foot at The Home Depot or Lowe's, to wrap around them. The insulation will keep hot air in the ducts, making your rooms feel toasty in winter. This effort can also save you around 10 percent on your heating bill.

Recycling Appliances Responsibly

Why recycle your appliances? For starters, consider that the average refrigerator 10 years or older contains more than 120 pounds of recyclable steel, meaning the energy saved by recycling one refrigerator is equal to the energy needed to run a new Energy Star–qualified refrigerator for 8 months. In addition, refrigerators and freezers contain refrigerants, oils and other compounds that, by federal law, must be removed and recovered before the metals and other selected parts can be recycled. So how do you recycle your appliances responsibly? Here are five ways:

1. Ask the retailer of your new refrigerator or freezer if it's willing to pick up and recycle your old ones. Best Buy, for example, will recycle your old unit for free if you buy a new refrigerator and receive basic delivery. Your favorite retailer may offer a similar program.

2. Check with your state energy office or local electric utility. Some states now require that you recycle used appliances as part of the American Recovery and Reinvestment Act of 2009. Some may also offer higher rebates for recycling. In addition, local utilities and energy-efficiency organizations support a growing number of refrigerator and freezer recycling programs. To locate offers from states and utilities, visit *energystar.gov/index. cfm?fuseaction=rebate.rebate_ locator*, enter your zip code, select the refrigerator/freezer box, and click the "Locate Special Offers/ Rebates" button.

3. Ask your municipality about the pickup of old appliances. Contact them directly for information as they may have specific requirements, such as the removal of CFCs before pickup.

4. Talk to your local scrap metal recycler. Thousands of scrap metal recyclers can recycle old fridges and freezers. To find one near you, visit the Steel Recycling Institute's website at: *recycle- steel.org/cgi-bin/sridbq3.pl*.

5. Donate your appliances to a charitable organization and get a tax deduction, too. A link on *DiggersList.com* allowed me to locate one of Habitat for Humanity's ReStores in my area, and the store was willing to come and pick up my old refrigerator and stove for free (proceeds from the sale of the appliances will help fund Habitat for Humanity projects around the country). Another way to dispose of your old appliances responsibly is to try to sell them directly through DiggersList. To find out more, visit *diggerslist.com*, or to donate to a ReStore through the site, go to *diggerslist.com/post/ donation/*.

Opposite: The owners of this 70-year-old home expanded it with several additions and improved its energy efficiency with new windows and doors. Left: A ceiling fan in the home's master bedroom reduces the need for air conditioning and cuts energy costs.

DIY Sealing and Insulation Help

A certain amount of fresh air coming into the home is necessary for good indoor air quality and building specifications set the minimum amount of fresh air needed for a house. For help on knowing whether you're sealing your home properly, consider these options:

• **The Department of Energy** offers an online DIY Guide to Sealing and Insulating that includes step-by-step instructions for sealing common air leaks and adding insulation to the attic. Visit *energystar.gov/index.cfm?c=diy. diy_index.*

• **The Energy–Star website** also offers recommended levels of insulation. Visit *energystar.gov. index.cfm?c=home_sealing.hm_ improvement_insulation_table.*

• **You can also hire a home energy rater,** who can help identify what kind of insulation or sealing you need, or enlist a contractor who can use special diagnostic tools to pinpoint and seal air leaks in your home. If your home is too tight, he might recommend an enhanced ventilation system.

After any home sealing project, have a heating and cooling technician check to make sure that your combustion appliances (gas- or oil-fired furnace, water heater and dryer) are venting properly. For additional information on indoor air quality issues, visit the EPA's website at *epa.gov/iaq/ homes/hip-front.html.*

Insulating your hot water heater and the hot water pipes running along the walls or ceilings can also save you energy. One way to do this is to surround the heater with a blanket of insulation, which you can purchase for $20 to $40 at Lowe's. Doing so may save you $100 annually on heating bills. Polystyrene tube insulation, which has a slit along the edge, slips right over the pipes. The insulation keeps the heat in the pipes longer, easing the effort for your hot water heater. This type of insulation costs 25 ¢ per foot at The Home Depot and can save you $50 on your heating bill.

• **Enhance your home's heating and cooling system.** There are a number of simple steps you can take to ensure your HVAC system operates at its best, which will help trim energy costs. Start by changing its filters regularly—at least monthly. Dirty filters force your system to work harder, which wastes energy and can add 10 to 30 percent to your energy bills.

Next, program or replace your thermostat. Set the thermostat to turn on any time the daytime temperature drops below, say, 68°F (it's cheaper to maintain a consistent temperature than to turn a thermostat up and down). If your thermostats aren't programmable, consider replacing them. They're easy to install and cost from $35 to $250—and you'll recover the cost in a month or two. You can save up to $100 a year by using a new setback thermostat.

Another energy-efficient option is to install a whole-house fan, which uses cool air in the evening to cool the entire house and push hot air out of the attic area. Ceiling fans or whole-house fans can help reduce your need to use the air conditioner.

Tip: In addition to helping you set the mood of a room, dimmers enable you to conserve energy and extend the life of your bulbs, too. The Skylark ecodim dimmer from Lutron Electronics, for example, is programmed to limit light levels to no more than 85 percent of full capacity at all times. The decrease in light level is imperceptible to the eye, but can reduce energy usage by 15 percent—more than doubling the life of an incandescent bulb.

A whole-house water filtration system, which treats water where the main water line enters the house, delivers bottle-quality water from all faucets and removes sediments that can cause harm to appliances that rely on water, such as dishwashers.

improving safety

Keeping your home safe from environmental pollutants also enhances its value. Here's a look at a few of the areas where the safety of your home can be enhanced with both low- and high-tech solutions, along with tips for making smart choices when renovating old homes.

• **Water filtration:** In addition to conservation, controlling the safety and quality of your drinking water is also important. In general, municipal water supplies in our country are of good quality and the tap water in our homes is safe to drink. But a few years, ago, the Natural Resources Defense Council (NRDC; *nrdc.org*) issued a report on tap water quality in 19 U.S. cities and five of them rated poor.

To get a sense of the water quality in your area, read your municipal water report. The Safe Water Act requires municipal agencies to issue a water quality report listing levels of detected contaminants in the water supply, which is sent to households once a year in their water bills. Even if your water is clean, it can pick up contaminants from pipes leading to or in the home.

If you can't replace your pipes, you can install a home water-treatment system that will improve the quality of the water, though no system eliminates all contaminants. Whole-house systems or point-of-entry systems treat water for the entire house where the main water line enters it. Point-of-use filters clean water from the fixture to which they are attached. Whole-house water filtration systems can handle much more water than a filtered pitcher sitting on your countertop. Another benefit of using a whole-house filter is that it can remove sediments as well as bad tastes and odors. Sediments can wreak havoc on your appliances, too, so hooking up a whole-house filtration system can save a lot of wear and tear on your washer, dryer, hot water heater, and more. Whole-house filters also remove chlorine from the water as it enters the water main, so it never enters the house itself. Chlorine can form chloroform gas from such everyday activities as taking a shower and flushing the toilet. Inhaling chloroform can lead to respiratory problems like bronchitis and asthma. Using a whole-house water filtration system will also give you bottled-water-quality water from every faucet in your house. Furthermore, your skin will feel softer after bathing because harmful chemicals are removed from the water, and you won't be inhaling gaseous chemicals while showering or running the dishwasher.

• **Ventilation and toxic substances:** Many home improvement projects involve introducing any number of toxic substances into your home,

Opposite and left: An automatic vacuum beneath the island in this kitchen eases cleanup. Cabinets with slightly different door styles in three finishes keep the room interesting, as do counter surfaces of soapstone and Bianco Romano granite (test granite for radon before purchasing if possible).

duced by incomplete combustion, and if enough of it attaches to your blood cells, your blood loses its ability to transport oxygen, and you suffocate. Carbon monoxide can be produced by many household appliances, such as gas ranges or stoves, gas clothes dryers, water heaters and furnaces. If household items like these are in poorly ventilated areas, carbon monoxide can build up, and before you know it, you're surrounded by toxic air that will poison you if you inhale it. You can install a carbon monoxide detector, which is a lot like a smoke detector, in the ceiling or get a plug-in version. Companies like Kidde or First Alert offer carbon monoxide detectors for under $40. Choose a detector that is UL-certified.

Asbestos: Asbestos is a naturally occurring mineral fiber that is heat-resistant and extremely durable. Because of these qualities, it became useful in construction and was commonly included in older houses. When it is crushed or unsealed, however, the fibers can be released and pose health risks, including lung cancer. As long as the surface in which they're contained is not damaged and is well sealed, the material is considered safe. To protect your home during a remodeling project, look at a document called "Asbestos in the Home" available online on the EPA's website at *epa. gov/asbestos/pubs/ashome.html.*

Radon: Radon is the second leading cause of lung cancer in the U.S. You can't see or smell it, but it can be contained in granite countertops or exist in the ground around your home. It's not hard to measure the level of radon in your home. For more information, see the EPA's "A Citizen's Guide to Radon," "Home Buyer's and Seller's Guide to Radon," and "Consumer's Guide to Radon Reduction" at *epa.gov/radon/pubs.*

Lead: About half the homes built before 1978 contain lead-based paint. Two out of three homes built between 1940 and 1960 have lead-based paint. Nine out of 10 homes built before 1940 have lead-based paint. If you're working on a home renovation, repair or painting project in a home built before 1978, then you need to know how to work safely with lead-based paint. If the lead in paint gets into the bodies of children, it can damage the nervous system and cause developmental and behavioral problems that can affect them for their lifetime. In adults, lead poisoning causes health and reproductive problems. If you're working on the home yourself, visit the EPA's website for more information at *epa.gov/oppt/lead/pubs/leadinfo.htm.* If you're working with a contractor, be sure he or she is certified to work on a home containing lead.

or disturbing those that are already there. If your project involves installing new cabinets, carpet, flooring or even furniture, be sure your home is properly ventilated, ideally leaving windows open for at least 72 hours after installation to reduce effects such as wheezing, sore throats and other reactions caused by the outgassing of volatile organic compounds from the materials and adhesives after they're installed. Some experts say that it can take up to a year before new products fully outgas.

Whether you're renovating or not, asbestos, radon, carbon monoxide and lead can contribute to unsafe living environments. To protect your family from the ill effects of these common toxic elements, consider taking some low-cost precautions.

Carbon Monoxide: Start by installing a carbon monoxide detector. Carbon dioxide (CO_2) and carbon monoxide (CO) are sometimes confused. They are quite different in their effects on humans.

Carbon dioxide (CO_2) is present in the atmosphere and the increase in its presence over the past few decades is due mostly to the burning of fuels such as coal, wood, oil and natural gas, especially coal. Almost all life is dependent on plants getting CO_2 from the atmosphere. Air can contain about 5 percent CO_2 before people become uncomfortable, and sensors are often built into HVAC systems to control the levels of CO_2 in the air.

Carbon monoxide, on the other hand, is a dangerous poison pro-

Below left: Recycling and waste bins are neatly stowed in an easy-access pullout unit. Below right: Porcelain accents on the hardware and shaped legs give the painted cabinets a furniture-like quality.

Opposite: A refrigerator wall is concealed behind custom cabinetry with a coffee and breakfast center sandwiched between. Drawers holding bowls and cereal make access easy for kids.

details that make a difference

When you're focused on the big picture, it's often easy to forget the subtle details or hidden elements of a home that add value and comfort. But things like doorstops, hardware with heft or beautifully framed art hung by a pro lend practicality and polish that boost the form and function of your home as well as your sense of well-being. If you need to stretch your dollars and are tempted to bypass the touches that can make your day-to-day routine more civilized, consider where you might make a trade-off—forgoing something you want but can live without to get something else that will truly enrich your daily experience. Or, use your ingenuity to creatively solve a problem with a little DIY effort to get the level of quality you desire.

When making choices for our kitchen renovation, for example, I really wanted a premium door style for the cabinets—it was warmer and richer looking than the standard grade. So we splurged on the doors and saved by purchasing an affordable refrigerator and mi-crowave to stay on budget. There were lots of other such choices my husband and I had to make during the course of our kitchen project, like paying a little extra to get a pro-grade range with sealed burners, but buying one of the more affordable models to stay on budget, and splurging on a made-to-order tile for the backsplash yet keeping it limited to a less-than-10-square-foot area to keep costs in check.

Another touch that makes our kitchen more comfortable and protects our investment in new cabinets is the installation of stays on the cabinet doors, which keep them from banging into and damaging the ones that are 90 degrees adjacent. These slim woven-wire cords, which cost practically nothing, wouldn't have occurred to me if I hadn't mentioned the problem to our contractor, John Loffredo, who figured out how to solve all kinds of other little problems I encountered as our renovation was underway. You'd be surprised how many of your conundrums can be easily solved by a pro or an expert at a home or hardware store if you simply ask.

decorating
getting started

Improving the quality and comfort of your home doesn't have to involve moving walls, renovating rooms or creating new additions. Decorative elements—from furniture and rugs to paint and wallpaper—can also transform the beauty and function of your rooms as well as the quality of your life.

Whether you're starting from scratch or building on an existing scheme, start by considering your home as a whole. The key to creating a harmonious environment is instilling a sense of continuity from room to room. To make your home feel integrated, keep the shell of your rooms—the walls, windows, ceilings and floors—consistent so that spaces seem to flow from one to another if it isn't uniform already. Consider installing the same flooring throughout the primary public spaces. Choose similar or matching fabrics for window treatments from room to room to keep spaces from feeling disjointed. And paint walls in neutral colors or colors that complement one another in tone to make them feel connected. If possible, keep molding, millwork and trims consistent throughout, too. Against a clean, consistent backdrop, the style of your furnishings will clearly resonate.

Any project is easier if you break it down into manageable parts, such as tackling one room at a time or establishing a game plan for getting things done in phases, such as first painting walls, then laying carpet, then reupholstering furniture, etc. If funds are limited, at least try to start with a good foundation of furniture in every room and layer in extras over time as your budget permits, so that you can make use of all the spaces in your home while you live in it. A room that falls dormant for lack of furnishing can become a dumping ground for odds and ends that have no place elsewhere in the house, and may never wind up materializing as a genuinely livable space.

upholstered furniture

A beautiful sofa or chair may delight the eye, but if it isn't comfortable, its value is instantly compromised. Before spending money on an upholstered piece with a look you love, be sure to test it for comfort. No one needs a good-looking piece of furniture that never gets used.

In addition to looking and feeling good, a good chair or sofa should be built to last. When shopping for upholstered pieces, ask what the frame is made of. Frames made of kiln-dried hardwoods like maple or ash will be more durable than those constructed of soft woods like pine or birch. And the frame should be secured with mortise-and-tenon joints or double dowels with corner blocks screwed into place. There are several levels of cushions, from pure polyfoam to a mix of polyfoam and fiber to feathers or down around a foam-

Cost Comparison

While a beautifully designed room can be furnished for upward of $100,000, the average cost of decorating a room in a standard American household is $10,000. Certainly, with savvy shopping and the creative use of flea-market finds, you can style a room for even less. But using $10,000 as a benchmark, furnishing a comfortable room costs about the same as a week's vacation for a family of four or the cost for six people to dine out at a fancy restaurant once a month for a year.

core. The polyfoam will be more affordable, hold its shape longer and be easier to maintain. Down cushions are super-comfortable, but need care and cost more.

case goods

Wood furnishings—from tables and consoles to dressers and armoires—collectively fall into a category known as case goods. Like wood doors or floors, wood furniture expands in moist environments and contracts in dry ones, and is therefore prone to splitting and cracking over time. To be sure any investment you make in wood furniture is sound, consider its construction and finish. High-quality case goods have dovetailed solid-wood panels. If the surface is covered with a veneer, the veneer is generally applied to an engineered wood base, such as MDF, which is dimensionally more stable than solid wood and doesn't warp or split. The veneer should be large and uniform with aligned grains. And the finish should be clear and deep to bring out the grain in the wood.

paint

Paint is a low-cost, high-impact way to improve the look of your rooms. But not all paints are alike. If you're simply refreshing an existing paint job with the same or a similar color, one coat of paint should suffice to cover up nicks and marks, and you can probably get away with using a low-cost paint to do the job. But if you're covering a darker color with a lighter one or changing to a completely different color, you'll need to apply a primer before the paint and then roll on two coats of paint to get the desired effect. In this case, you're better off going with a higher quality paint, or you may have to return to the paint store to buy more paint and wind up paying more in the end anyhow.

Painting is an easy DIY project, and you can also save money by doing it yourself. But if your walls are cracked or damaged, or your current paint is peeling, investing in the help of a pro who has the skill and tools to handle repairs and skim coating will be worth every penny. Labor costs vary by region, but a simple paint job with no repair work might cost around $250 per room, depending on its size and not including the paint. If you're planning to paint a ceiling, be sure to purchase ceiling paint, which is formulated to cover more absorbent surfaces.

bedding

Comfortable and attractive sheets are more affordable than ever, with manufacturers offering a diverse selection of colors, patterns and trims for every budget. And a new set of sheets can not only freshen the look of your bedroom but also help you sleep better.

• **Fiber:** Cotton is by far the most popular fabric for sheets. Because of their long fibers (also known as staples), the highest quality cotton varieties are Sea Island cotton, grown off the East Coast of the United States; Egyptian cotton, grown in Egypt; and Pima cotton, grown in the U.S. Even if sheets are made with a small percentage of these high-quality fibers, they can be identified as Egyptian, Pima or Sea Island cotton. So check labels carefully and look for a high percentage—Supima Cotton is a trademark that indicates the fibers are 100 percent Pima cotton.

Environmentally friendly bed linens are also becoming popular

How Much Paint Do I Need?

The websites of many paint companies have calculating tools that can help you determine how much paint you'll need. But bear in mind that they will supply you with an amount sufficient to cover walls with one coat of paint, so you may need to double the amount if you're changing your walls to a completely different color.
You can also use the following instructions to help you determine how much paint you'll need.

1. Measure the width of your walls and multiply by their height to calculate the number of square feet of space that will be coated.

2. Subtract the square footage of openings, such as archways, windows and doors, that won't be covered by paint.

3. Divide the number of square feet to be covered by the number of square feet that a gallon of your particular brand of paint can cover. (A gallon of Sherwin-Williams Harmony brand of paint, for example, covers 350 square feet. If you were to coat 1,000 square feet with this paint, you'd divide 1,000 by 350 to get 2.86 gallons, and would need to purchase 3 gallons of paint to do the job.)

Home Economics

Here's the kind of paint you can get at different price points:

Good—up to $20 a gallon: Basic latex paint with fewer additives that provide moisture or mildew resistance.
Better—up to $30 a gallon: These paints offer higher durability and better stain resistance than lower–quality paints.
Best—up to $55 a gallon: Usually made with the highest–quality pigments, these often thick, one-coat paints allow you to get the job done faster and can be antimicrobial and eco-friendly.

and easier to find. Certified organic cotton has the same properties as conventional cotton, but is grown without the use of pesticides, insecticides or chemical fertilizers. Bamboo is a soft, breathable fiber made from renewable bamboo grass. Bamboo sheets are naturally resistant to bacteria and can wick away moisture. Some sheets are made with fiber from beech trees, which are grown on sustainable farms. The fiber is often marketed under the brand name Tencel. Both bamboo and beech can be blended with cotton for increased durability.

Home Economics

The price of sheets is determined by the fabric, weave and thread count. Sheets usually come in sets, which include a fitted bottom sheet, a flat sheet and two pillowcases. Here's what you can expect to pay for a full-price queen set:

Good—$40 to $70: Cotton-polyester blends or 100 percent cotton with a thread count of up to 250. Some 100 percent cotton flannel or jersey sheets also fall into this price range.

Better—$70 to $130: 100 percent cotton percale in a 300 to 400 thread count. You can also find some 230-thread-count bamboo sets.

Best—$130 to $190: 400- to 600-thread-count Egyptian or Pima cotton, some with windowpane or hemstitch detailing.

Ultra—$190 and higher: At this price level, sheets and pillowcases are sold individually and often imported. Thread counts are from 600 to more than 1,000, in 100 percent Egyptian or Supima cotton.

• **Weave:** Sheets are made in several different types of weaves. Here's a rundown of the options:
percale—a closely woven plain weave with a silklike feel
sateen—has more yarn on the surface and a softer, more lustrous hand
flannel—a brushed cotton with a napped finish and a cozy, fuzzy feel
jersey—a flat cotton knit often used for T-shirts

• **Thread count:** The thread count of a sheet is determined by the number of threads lengthwise (called the warp) and widthwise (called the weft) in a 1-inch square of fabric. Generally, the higher the thread count, the softer the sheet. A decade or so ago, a 300-thread-count sheet was considered quite luxurious. Now sheets with a thread count of 600, 800 and even more than 1,000 are easy to find, but often quite expensive.

Thread count isn't the only indicator of softness. The ply, or number of threads wrapped together, as well as fiber choice makes a difference, too. Bamboo and beech sheets, for example, often have a lower thread count because the fibers are naturally softer and silkier. Also, softer sheets with a high thread count, such as sateens, which are very light and thin, might not be as durable as sheets in other weaves and thread counts. For all intents and purposes sheets with a 250 thread count are soft enough for most people.

• **Size and shape:** It's important that sheets fit your mattress as well as possible. Fitted sheets that are too loose will twist and bunch up; those that are too tight can ride up the sides of the mattress and pop off the corners. Aside from offering a neat appearance, a sheet that fits well provides a smooth sleeping surface, greater comfort and a better chance for uninterrupted sleep.

Sheets come in twin, extra-long twin, full, queen, king and California king sizes to correspond to your mattress. Pillow tops and Euro-tops have also made mattresses deeper than ever, so be sure to measure your mattress depth before shopping for sheets and check package labels. The depth of standard sheets is 7 to 9 inches, deep sheets are 10 to 15 inches, and extra-deep are 15 to as much as 22 inches.

The package label also should indicate whether the elastic on the fitted sheet can be found all around the edges, which is preferable, or just on the corners. Elastic that encircles the sheet provides a snugger fit, reduces bagginess and increases the comfort factor.

Tip: Now that bedbugs are commonplace again, it's worth protecting your mattress with a cover that prevents the critters from hiding out in the seams around the edges. A $50 to 100 investment can spare you the hassle of replacing an infested mattress and minimize the grief and expense of extermination. One brand recommended by pest controllers is Mattress Safe.

Protect furnishings by polishing wooden architectural elements and case goods with a little natural beeswax once or twice a year, regularly vacuuming upholstered pieces and window treatments, and conditioning leather pieces.

protecting your investments

To preserve the value of any investment you make in your home, maintenance is key. A little TLC and minimal monetary outlay on a regular basis can save a bundle on repairing or replacing costly furnishings or architectural elements down the road. An ounce of prevention, as the saying goes, is worth a pound of cure.

• **Furniture:** If you take care of your furnishings, they can last a lifetime—and sometimes even improve with age. Make it simple for family and friends to respect furniture by always topping wood tables with placemats or tablecloths for every meal and having coasters on hand in gathering spaces, such as living rooms, family rooms and sun rooms. If you employ a housekeeper, make sure he or she handles your furniture with care, too. The following practical advice will help you preserve both hard and soft furnishings.

Wood furniture: Dust wood furniture with a damp cloth and dry immediately with a chamois or other soft cloth. Use commercial wood cleaning products sparingly if at all. Protect wood furnishings from damage caused by moisture, heat and sunlight by positioning them away from windows, radiators or forced-air heating elements. And never place anything hot or wet on a wood surface. If you do damage wood furniture with heat or water rings or stains, you can make it disappear with a stain- and ring-removing cloth from the Jasco Chemical Company, which costs about $4 and works miracles. Affix felt or leather pads beneath table lamps to keep them from scratching wood tables. Polish wood pieces with just a little natural beeswax (too much will cloud the finish) a couple of times a year. To enable sticky wooden dresser drawers to slide open smoothly, run a white candle over the glides.

Soft furnishings and upholstery: Flip and fluff cushions once a week or as needed, and vacuum the surface of curtains, shades and chair cushions with a brush attachment once a week. Use the narrow suction attachment to vacuum in the crevices of chairs and sofas, too. Immediately blot spills with a white cloth. Then follow by blotting with another white cloth dampened with distilled water and then again with a dry one to remove any stain. Never rub upholstery or fabric with a textured cloth or you may damage the finish or drive the stain in deeper. Draw curtains or shades during the day if possible to prevent sunlight from fading fabrics. Keep leather pieces from drying out and cracking by rubbing them with leather condi-

Opposite, left and bottom: Using the brush attachment on the hose of a vacuum cleaner to clean curtains and shades will keep them fresh and prolong their life. If necessary, a professional cleaning service can remove the window treatments and dry-clean them or steam or spot-clean on site. Drawing curtains and shades during the sunniest times of day will help keep furnishings from fading.

tioner now and then. And consider having upholstered pieces professionally cleaned once or twice a year.

• **Windows:** When done regularly, washing windows helps prevent them from becoming stained, pitted or etched by dirt and grime. If you live in an area with especially wet climate conditions, consider cleaning your windows two to four times a year. In drier conditions, once a year inside and out can suffice, unless you smoke in your home or have small children or pets. In these cases, you may need window maintenance on a regular basis.

Cleaning windows is a fairly simple DIY project, but professional window cleaning is really quite affordable, at around $10 per pane for windows without muntins. Pros will also have the tools and supplies to handle problem areas or second-story or tall windows, sparing you the time and trouble of scrubbing and razoring if need be to clear the pores of any dirt or paint and over-spraying to make them smooth again. Pros will often remove screens and clean them and their frame, and clean window tracks and sills as well. They will

also clean without leaving streaks or residue behind. If you have tinted windows, do not use any products containing ammonia. And if you have a fogged window, it is the result of a broken seal, caused by the settling of your house's foundation or extreme changes in weather. Pros can also check for faulty seals and provide advice for solving this problem.

• **Wood floors:** Replacing a wood floor is costly. Refinishing one isn't cheap either, and doing so is extremely messy to boot. So it pays to protect your wood floor to prevent having to face either of these choices. I'm a fan of the Bona floor care system, which involves three steps. First, you dustmop the floor with a fluffy white removable electrostatic pad once a week or as needed. Then, using the same mop, you clean using a microfiber pad and an eco-friendly cleaning solution that leaves no dulling residue. Both pads are washable, making the floor care system even more eco-friendly. Finally, once or twice a year, you polish the floor with another microfiber pad that looks a little like sheepskin and Bona's hardwood floor polish, which restores and enhances the finish with a touch of urethane. This pad also works with the same mop. To keep your furniture from scratching your floor, use self-stick felt floor-care pads from 3M or any other company under the feet of chairs, armoires and tables.

If you find that you do need to repair a damaged wood floor, find out from a flooring pro if you can buff the floor rather than sand. Buffing skims the surface of the floor with fine sandpaper and generally requires only one coat of polyurethane to refinish the floor; it might cost about $2 per square foot, though rates vary widely by region and firm. A full sand completely removes the surface with two or three levels of sandpaper, requires two or three coats of polyurethane to finish and might cost about $3.50 per square foot. Bona also offers a floor refinishing service, which includes a superior dust containment system that will ease your life enormously—as cleaning the resulting dust from walls and ceilings and any curtains that aren't fully covered during the process is another tedious aspect of the project.

Tip: Replace mismatched hangers with the flat, flocked versions you can buy at Bed Bath & Beyond and other home stores. Not only do they allow me to hang my clothes in one line, making them easier to sort through, their slim profile allows me to more than double the storage capacity of a closet.

A Word on Storage

Before embarking on my home improvement projects, I was committed to clearing out some clutter and organizing my closets. The first step I took was to consult Lisa Zaslow, the CEO and founder of New York–based Gotham Organizers.

Though my husband wouldn't necessarily agree with her, she told me that compared with most of the clients she sees I am actually amazingly neat. "Even the clutter you have is neat," she said. "It's squared off in nice straight piles, which all contain similar items." Most of my clutter comes in the form of books and magazines—due to the nature of my business—and I fall into the category of people that Lisa calls "pilers," as opposed to "filers." Here are three of her tips on how to get organized:

1. Create an intuitive effective filing system with color-coded folders and clear labels. "Organizing your papers is one of the easiest ways to improve your productivity and reduce stress," she says.

2. Become a filer rather than a piler. "All you need to do to go from a being piler to a filer is to turn your piles 90 degrees and put them on shelves so you can easily access them," she told me. To do this, we installed some new built-in bookshelves, which we created space for by converting an underused linen closet into a built-in bookshelf and using IKEA's Pax system to turn a section of a closet in our guest room into a shelving area for books, magazines, and crafts and sewing supplies. We also installed other components of a Pax system in our hall closet, enabling part of it to serve as utility storage for tools, documents, lightbulbs and gardening supplies, and the other part to house coats, hats, scarves and other gear.

3. Maximize prime closet real estate. According to Lisa, this is the area in a closet that falls between the shoulders and the hips and is the easiest zone to access. In our closets, this area was sitting empty. If we were to put shelves in the closets along this area, she told me, we'd have room for even more stuff (just what we don't want!). Though we eliminated a fair amount of unnecessary stuff, we did follow Lisa's advice, and in addition to the Pax systems we installed in our coat closet and guest room closet, we also installed storage systems from California Closets to max out the vertical real estate in our wardrobe closets. My system includes drawers, shelves, hanging rods and shoe cubbies that easily accommodate all of the clothes I have left after weeding out a bunch of stuff and donating it to The Salvation Army.

renovate

1ife changes, and sometimes a house has to change along with it. We all want a home that fits our lifestyle—one that feels just right. But often, old houses—whether built 50 or 150 years ago—just don't work for the way we live today. Sometimes even relatively new houses need to be adapted to suit a growing family or stylistic point of view. The projects on the following pages show how several homeowners renovated their homes to accommodate a variety of different needs.

Some are whole-house renovations, involving reconfigured rooms and additions. Others are transformations of single rooms, which often involved breaking down walls and co-opting space from adjoining areas to gain more room. And a few involved complete makeovers within an existing footprint. Most of these remodels include new fixtures, finishes and fittings, but many recycle parts of the room's past, too. Whether public gathering spaces or private comfort zones, all began with clearly defined goals and a game plan for achieving them.

fresh start

Reality: Built in 1925, Jeff and Tray Schlarb's three-story 2,500-square-foot house in San Francisco's Marina District had been occupied by the same owner for more than 50 years before they bought it. Only the kitchen had been remodeled—once, in 1975. Inside, the four-bedroom, three-bath home was a jumble of frilly curtains, Mediterranean-style arches, and ornate crown moldings—completely the opposite of the crisp, clean look favored by the couple, who co-own and run Green Couch, a home staging, decorating and remodeling business.

Dream: Clean, efficient family-friendly interiors.

Making it manifest: Awaiting the birth of their first child, the Schlarbs were attracted to the house's location in one of the city's few flat neighborhoods (a real bonus when wrangling a newborn). Its close proximity to water and its wide, elegant proportions were other strong pluses. Though the interiors did not reflect their tastes, they saw nothing but potential. Here's how they transformed the parts they didn't like:

1. They started by updating the infrastructure. Collaborating with San Francisco architect Seth Brookshire, they redid the plumbing and electrical systems and installed new radiant-floor heating, which doesn't kick dust into the air the way forced-air systems do. Then they fearlessly stripped all three floors of all architectural ornaments and moldings.

2. The next step was to open some spaces and enclose others. On the main floor, they opened up a wall separating the dining room and kitchen to create a more contemporary floor plan and bring in more natural light. Upstairs, they enclosed an illegal deck, which had been built by the previous owner, to accommodate a spacious new master bath. They also turned the original master bath and closet into a nursery.

3. Once the layout was amended to suit the young family's lifestyle, they turned their attention to the finishes and furniture. With a baby on the way, the couple wanted to incorporate as many green, nontoxic, healthy materials as possible. So, they specified non-VOC paints and stains throughout the house They also ruled out wall-to-wall carpeting in favor of easy-to-clean wood floors made of dark-stained walnut planks.

4. The couple also opted to keep surfaces and architectural elements simple, neutral and clean. Because they work with color all day long in other people's rooms, they wanted their own interiors to be restful and calm. "I wanted to go back to a simple, airy white space to declutter my head," says Tray. To achieve this goal, they skillfully repeated materials and colors from room to room to eliminate any sense of visual chaos. For example, they painted all the walls the same shade of soft gray-tinged-white throughout the house, allowing the serene spirit to flow from room to room. They also installed the dark wood flooring everywhere except the bathrooms, which also unifies the spaces on all three levels. In each of the baths they included the same style of custom cabinetry for vanity storage. And they limited window treatments to plantation shutters and solar shades to keep the ambience really crisp.

5. In addition to limiting the palette to mostly white, chocolate brown and a few neutrals, the couple used accent colors and patterns judiciously, relying mostly on geometrics in shades of yellow, dusty pink and pale blue.

design details

Jeff and Tray Schlarb make their living by giving rooms instant style to sell homes fast. While this home underwent a substantial remodel, the decorative elements do much to shape the spirit of the rooms, too. Here are three of the couple's quick-change strategies:

• Create instant visual interest and style by pairing opposites, such as new and vintage furnishings, for example, or contrasting materials, such as rough wood and shiny chrome.

• Add polish with window treatments and plants. "These are the two things that make a room feel finished," says Jeff.

• Focus on the walls you see first. "You always want a good view facing you when you turn a corner and walk into a room," says Jeff. "Try to create impact and balance on that wall."

new life

Reality: With its French country–lite style, arched windows and pale-pink brick facade, the long-empty '60s house was out of character in its Lake Michigan vacation community. Inside, the house was dark, with outdated finishes and shag carpet. But it was positioned nicely on a beautiful lot.

Dream: A warm, rustic weekend retreat.

Making it manifest: Embarking on a yearlong renovation before they moved into the house, owners Tim Scott and Jeff Welch retained its footprint, but reconfigured the roof and stripped the house down to its studs, keeping the existing windows but giving the home a completely different character more in tune with its environs. These were important first steps, but the owners, who have two children and three dogs, realized that after removing a bedroom to make a double-height dining space, their initial stab at a remodel wasn't quite working. Two bedrooms made it difficult for them to accommodate guests, and the living space was insufficient. Furthermore, the dogs were scuffing the pine floors, and the windows were too small to let in light and views. So they brought in architect John Hurst, of J. Hurst & Associates, Fennville, Michigan, to plan the changes they wanted. Here's a breakdown of the steps they took over the course of the two remodels to get their dream house:

1. Step one involved revamping the surfaces inside and out. The exterior brick was replaced with cedar siding, interior walls were removed to create an open plan, and walls, ceilings and floors were surfaced with pine. The bedroom above the dining area was eliminated to create a two-story ceiling, and the kitchen was gutted and remodeled.

2. Next, they enlarged the footprint. To give the homeowners more space, the architect bumped out the rear wall 8 feet and replaced the screened porch with a four-season sunroom. The addition also provided the foundation for the upstairs floor space they needed to add a spacious master bath.

3. The old windows were all replaced with larger, energy-efficient models, which meant ripping out much of the siding and paneling installed in the first remodel.

4. Revamping the kitchen made it much more functional and hospitable. The extra first-floor square footage gave Hurst

room to reconfigure and reorient the kitchen, giving it a wall of windows and deck access.

5. The entry was made more welcoming, too. A small bump-out at the front door gave definition to the entry hall and provided room above to expand the guest bath.

6. Introducing low-maintenance surfaces made the home easier to live in. Throughout most of the house, pine floors were replaced with concrete tiles, set in a staggered pattern. "They're easy to care for and they're dog-friendly," says Jeff.

7. The master suite was also expanded and improved. Enlarged to encompass the area defined by the sunroom below, the comfortable master suite, which previously contained only a tiny closet and a one-person bath, now includes lots of sunlight, space and amenities.

8. A new private guest suite built above the garage allows the family to comfortably entertain visitors, while allowing them private quarters of their own.

design details

• Decorative touches, such as colorful ceramic vases and vintage wooden birdhouses, complement the country spirit of the house.

• A substantial collection of folk art adds whimsy and punches of color to the decor of every room.

• Recycled furniture and flea-market finds bring warmth and relaxed comfort to the spacious rooms.

• Variegated tile work and painted beadboard bring splashes of color to the baths.

rooms with views

Reality: Kathy and Tom Cotney's small two-story cottage was ideally situated on a woodsy hillside in northeastern Georgia's lake country. The 1960s cabin, which had been renovated in the '80s, included a master bedroom addition that jutted out from the back of the cabin's second floor. Inside, an open living area gave the family plenty of public space, but extra private spaces and service rooms were needed. And the interior was paneled in unpainted wood, which dimmed the interiors, while small windows overlooking the surrounding trees outside limited the room's sunlight and access to views.

Dream: A relaxing getaway with updated amenities and access to light and views.

Making it manifest: Delighted that the cottage didn't look like a typical in-town Atlanta house transplanted to the woods, the owners got in touch with friend and designer Craig Kettles of C Designs in Lakemont, Georgia, to help them refashion the house into the stress-free getaway they imagined. With Craig on board, they launched into a six-month remodeling effort that included gutting the interior and enhancing the house throughout to expand light and views. Here's how it was done:

1. The designer started the project by maximizing views. He replaced small metal windows with new, larger ones to take advantage of views.

2. Next he installed new wall paneling in the interior spaces. The living area configuration remained the same, but Kettles replaced the existing paneling with horizontal boards and had them painted cloud white.

3. New floors add warmth in keeping with the spirit of the house. Heart-pine floors replaced the old ones, which had buckled.

4. The kitchen got an update, including the usual amenities and new appliances plus an island for storage and extra seating and serving space.

5. Breathing room was introduced by doubling the first-floor living area. What had been open space below the master bedroom addition is now enclosed to house an entry hall, den, bathroom and laundry room.

6. Guest areas were enhanced, too. Upstairs, all guest rooms now open to a screened porch with stunning views of Lake Burton. The second floor was also reconfigured to include three baths. In addition to the regular bedrooms, there's also a compact bunkroom, which sleeps four extra guests.

design details

• Woven-reed window shades control light and privacy while remaining in keeping with the spirit of the house.

• A picket railing around the deck was replaced with open crossbeams to expand the view of the lake.

• Introducing new wall panels and painting the ones in the bedrooms white brightened what had been dim interiors.

• New built-in seating beneath the stairs maxes out usable space and provides a nice spot for a nap or reading a book.

An L-shaped island effectively divides the kitchen into working and eating zones and ensures the cook always has two working surfaces at hand.

country sophisticate

Reality: When recalling the old 14x9-foot kitchen in her 1920s brick colonial home in River Forest, Illinois, homeowner Nicole Bukers Jenkins describes it simply as "a dark, horrid place."

Dream: A clean, elegant, expanded space that would evoke the atmosphere of an estate property, yet with a modern sensibility.

Making it manifest: To create the gracious, traditional but not stuffy space she craved, the homeowner worked with Chicago-based kitchen designer Jean Stoffer, who knew the effect would be difficult to achieve within the confines of the existing kitchen. Determined to deliver on her client's dreams, however, the designer resolved the issues. Here's how she did it:

1. She began by moving an exterior wall 8 feet out. This breakthrough in the design process not only yielded more area in the room, but when fitted with a bank of south facing windows, brought in plenty of mood-lifting daylight, too. "Now, even when there's just a hint of a ray of sun, the room just explodes with light," says Stoffer.

2. To brighten the space, the designer introduced a wide range of light-reflective surfaces throughout. Stepped counters of stainless steel surround the main sink. Polished marble tops the L-shaped island. On the sink backsplash, glass mosaics shine, as do the glazed ceramic tiles that line the cooking alcove. And polished marble on the floors is studded with pewter insets for extra shine.

3. To give the space a living-area quality, the designer also controlled the appearance of appliances. Two refrigerators were faced with cabinet panels and made to look built-in, while the stove's antique-y appearance complements the kitchen's country manor look. Though the appliance is available in several colors, the designer opted for neutral stainless steel to give the owner more design flexibility in the future.

4. A mix of furniture-like cabinetry lends warmth and the feeling of a room that has evolved over time. The base cabinets along the windowed wall and around the stove are painted white, while those in the island are stained chocolate brown. Since conventional wall cupboards were not included in the room because they would obstruct the flow of light, the designer created a walk-in pantry to house the owner's staples and supplies.

Clockwise from top left: Deep-set windows and varying counter heights give the room dimensionality. A trio of fun pendants brightens the area over the island. A "dish dresser" with pullout serving boards holds serveware near the plating point of the island. A mix of tile on the backsplash behind the range adds panache. An old-world-style range in modern stainless steel anchors the cooking alcove. Decorative pewter inset tiles in the marble floor play off cabinet hardware. One of the two refrigerators on the sink wall is covered with cabinet doors for a furniture-like appearance.

5. A custom-designed armoire-like unit was installed to house dishes. Stoffer calls this storage element a "dish dresser," which sits against the back wall of the room. Its weathered-mirror doors are perfectly positioned to bounce sun around the space.

design details

• Architectural features dovetail with the rest of the house. The arched opening that frames the niche for the range, for example, repeats an architectural feature found throughout the house.

• The designer also credits the owner with bringing a strong style sense of her own to the kitchen project. The apple-green chinoiserie wallcovering and the sparkly pendant lights are two of her contributions, which give the room its distinctive, personal feel.

• Boosting the furniture-like treatment of the cabinets is unique drawer hardware in a variety of styles, from bin pulls to knobs to articulated handles.

high-performance hub

Reality: The builder-grade kitchen in Kathryn Griesinger and Lino Piedra's second home, a duplex in Vail, Colorado, was small with a semicircular counter that swooped into the adjoining living room and a stove that faced the entrance. "I didn't want people to open the front door and have the sink be the first thing they see," explains Lino, a former auto-industry executive who has dined in the world's finest restaurants, studied at Le Cordon Bleu and taken private lessons with renowned chefs around the globe.

Dream: A spacious, high-performance kitchen fit for gourmets, who frequently entertain.

Making it manifest: To reconfigure the space, the couple enlisted designer Mikal Otten of Exquisite Kitchen Design in Denver. "They wanted a fabulous kitchen for entertaining that included room for a large stove with two ovens for Lino, and a separate sous chef space with refrigerator and freezer drawers for Kathryn, who prepares salads and desserts," says Otten. Here are the steps he took to create a kitchen that served their very specialized needs:

1. Otten started the process by removing a wall and eliminating an office to make way for the laundry list of gourmet food-prep necessities. He also co-opted adjoining space to expand the volume.

2. The designer also planned distinct zones for efficiency and ease. Both food prep stations feature sinks—hers designed for cleaning veggies and his for power-washing pots and pans—as well as customized utensil drawers and individual dishwashers. "Two dishwashers are essential to good kitchen design because complex cooking generates more dishes, pots and pans than one machine can handle," says Lino, who claims the other essential ingredient is a strong exhaust system. "You don't want your house smelling like fish or bacon," he adds.

3. Since the kitchen is intended for entertaining, the designer incorporated a perch for guests. A counter on Lino's side provides a spot where guests can sit, set down a drink and chat with the chef.

4. He also merged high style with low maintenance. Aesthetically, the 275-square-foot kitchen is a contemporary surprise inside a decidedly Arts-and-Crafts-style package. The easy-to-clean vanilla glass cabinets, smooth blue pearl granite counters that can handle

Clockwise from top left: The bar-area countertop is made of blue pearl granite. The aluminum backsplash supports a stainless steel rail that provides easy access to utensils. In the second prep area, lower cabinets are made of horizontal-grain black oak with integrated aluminum handles, and upper cabinets are white, some fronted with frosted-glass doors. Under-counter fridge and freezer drawers provide a handy spot for stowing vegetables. A wine fridge is conveniently located near the bar. The custom drawer dividers organize utensils in the Alno cabinets. One of the sinks features a commercial-style faucet.

a hot pot, and sleek stainless appliances are better suited to the demands of a cook's kitchen.

design details

• To tie the modern design to the rest of the house, Otten kept the existing knotty alder window frames and added black oak cabinets to integrate with the dark pine floors in the adjacent living room.

• A planning perk that enhances the traffic flow is the placement of the wine cooler and coffeemaker, with cups and glasses conveniently stowed above, across from the counter. "Guests can help themselves to a cup of coffee or a glass of wine and take a seat without ever getting in the way of the cooks," says Otten.

• The revised floor plan allows for an additional food prep area with a second sink and dishwasher opposite the cooking and entertaining zone. The U-shaped layout of the cooking/bar area allows the owner to be at the stove and interact with guests at the same time.

Opposite: Painted Shaker-style cabinet doors from Brookhaven give the kitchen an appearance that is both classic and modern. Oak open shelves provide a note of warm contrast.

Right: A 24-inch Bertazzoni pro-grade range and 27-inch-wide Summit fridge make efficient use of the compact space. The engineered quartz countertop is eco-friendly. The floor tiles from Country Floors qualify for LEED points.

small wonder

Reality: In the New York City apartment I share with my husband, Anil, our 21-year-old 8-x-8-foot kitchen included builder-grade white laminate cabinets and counters that were beginning to crumble beneath the sink and around the dishwasher. Bland brown 8-inch-square tiles covered the floor. The microwave was broken and an oversize refrigerator cramped the tight space. Since the kitchen had a pass-through to the adjoining dining area and was visible from the living room, I wanted recessed-panel cabinets that would harmonize with the other millwork in our home and give the space a classic residential feel, yet still look modern.

Dream: More warmth, storage, counter space, efficiency and eco-friendliness within an existing compact footprint.

Making it manifest: As a long-time design editor, I've seen a lot of kitchen appliances and materials, so I was clear about the kind of cabinets, surfaces and fixtures I wanted. I did my own search for materials and appliances, and was fortunate to collaborate with several companies who were willing to sponsor my efforts with donated product, or support them by offering trade discounts. To execute the layout and the design of the kitchen, my husband and I worked with Dave Burcher, design director of Inhouse Kitchen Bath Home in New York City, who offered expert technical advice that I would have been lost without. Here's a rundown of what we did to create the kitchen we wanted:

1. We started by completely gutting the existing space. With the exception of the overhead light fixture and the dishwasher, which was only five years old and fully functional (if short on high design), we eliminated everything in the kitchen. To be as eco-friendly as possible, however, we donated the operable appliances and countertop to Habitat for Humanity's ReStore, and I gave one of the existing cabinets to our contractor, who was able to reuse it.

2. To gain breathing room and counter space, we opted for small-scale appliances. We chose a 24-inch pro-style range, which we splurged on, and a basic 27-inch counter-depth fridge, which we saved on. We entertain quite frequently, and the energy-efficient appliances, while compact, are more than adequate for our needs.

3. We also reconfigured the galley-style space, making it U-shaped to gain more storage and function. By adding shallow base cabinets at the dead end of the galley, we gained some extra counter space and squeezed in a storage zone below to house the wastebasket and recyclables. Open shelves above provide a pretty focal point at the far end of the kitchen.

4. Eco-friendly high-value cabinets add warmth and function. By building up the wall and installing cabinets that rise to the ceiling on one side of the kitchen, we gained a little more storage space. The cabinets feature soft-close drawers, pullout shelves and utensil dividers for enhanced functionality and ease of use. The oak finish of the open shelves offers a touch of contrast to the mostly white kitchen, and ties into the oak floors and windowsills in other parts of our home.

5. I wanted the kitchen to be as eco-friendly as possible, so we included a low-maintenance engineered quartz countertop

called Eco that was supplied by Cosentino. It keeps the scheme clean and crisp, is heat- and stain-resistant, and doesn't require sealing. The wood-look floor tiles we chose are the first and only tiles made that qualify for points from the U.S. Green Building Council's Leadership in Energy and Environmental Design (LEED) program. The glass tiles on the backsplash were made to order in the U.S.

6. A water-conserving faucet adds to the eco-friendliness. The swiveling faucet with pullout spout contributed by Elkay provides a clean profile that doesn't obstruct sight lines into the space and was designed specifically to complement the sink.

7. In a tiny space, every inch of breathing room counts. To foster a sense of openness without losing the cocooned feeling I like in the kitchen, we lowered the bar-height section of the countertop to create one expansive plane and open the pass-through. We also shaved off about 8 inches of a wall framing the entrance to the kitchen to match the depth of the counters and expand the operable width of the space.

design details

• From a *feng shui* perspective, the blue and charcoal gray tiles we chose just so happened to be appropriate colors for this area in our home, according to Katherine Lewis, an expert I consulted halfway through the design process. Based on advice from Lewis and Atsushi Shono, another *feng shui* expert I consulted, we also moved the position of the sink so that it didn't align directly with the stove.

• Our cabinet installer added wire stays on the cabinet doors that open at 90 degrees to adjacent cabinets. These thoughtful details keep the doors from hyperextending and the handles from banging into the adjoining cabinets.

• Thanks to a contribution from IKEA, door hardware harmonizes with the lines of the faucet, while a mix of decorative dishes, vases, serving pieces and cookware complements the clean Scandinavian spirit of the room.

• We chose a premium door panel for the cabinets, which features wider rails and stiles that lend the doors a sense of richness and substance. Speaker cloth on one of the cabinets placed below the countertop on the dining room side allows us to conceal a stereo woofer within.

• A metal grid protects the bottom of the stainless steel sink, while a cutting board, cut to fit, rests neatly and securely on top and extends the counter surface area as needed.

Opposite left: Elkay's low-flow Avado faucet swivels and includes an integrated extendable spray head. A bottom grid designed for the sink protects the base of the Elkay's sink from dings and scratches, and a cutting board also from Elkay fits precisely over the sink to extend the countertop if needed. Opposite, right: Glossy blue brick-shaped backsplash tiles provide a hint of color. This page: Pullout shelves allow easy access to pots and pans. Door and drawer hardware is from IKEA.

Opposite: A wall-mounted faucet saves precious space in the compact bath. The portion of the wall-spanning counter above the commode is removable for access to the tank for service. Right: A super-insulated window teamed with a towel warmer keeps the room toasty in cold weather.

country charm

Reality: The compact bath in designer Ingrid Leess's Connecticut home had character—vintage jade-green tiles climbed halfway up the walls and a stately old pedestal sink stood on one side with the original medicine cabinet mounted overhead. But its period look had long passed its prime. And the small room also sorely lacked sufficient storage space. Furthermore the top of the toilet tank had been pressed into service as a makeshift shelf—a risky scenario, given the slipperiness of the narrow surface. The pedestal sink had only enough set-down space to hold soap and a drinking cup. And a little side table had been edged into the room, but it was too low to reach comfortably, making it more of an awkward addition than an asset.

Dream: An airy, fresh space filled with plenty of easy-to-access storage and personal touches.

Making it manifest: When planning the remodel for the inefficient room, Leess started by righting all the storage wrongs, then adding all-new fixtures and surfaces. These are the steps she took to transform the tiny space:

1. She designed a new custom sink console that is much more useful than the ad hoc arrangement that previously existed. A shallow vessel sink sits on a quartz counter, which has "wings" extending to the side walls. This continuous surface is supported by turned-wood, crackle-finish legs, which are actually balusters salvaged from the designer's parents' home. Over the wall-mounted faucet, a 4-inch-wide ledge that's ideal for small decorative displays also runs the length of the room.

2. She also added a pair of tall mirrored cabinets to flank a wood-framed vintage mirror. She hung them so that when both are opened, they create a three-way mirror effect, which is great for styling hair and putting on makeup.

3. Next, the designer replaced old fixtures with compact new ones. To make the space more usable, she chose the smallest toilet available. With the old commode, a person's knees practically knocked against the tub, which itself was a space-wasting corner model. So a new conventional tub took its place.

4. She also redid all the finishes. Taking her Connecticut farmhouse's casual atmosphere into account, the designer used planked panels to cover the walls and installed them parallel to the floor to stretch the space visually. White marble mosaics are found on the floor, on the backsplash and in the storage niche in the shower. Their variegated tones and uneven edges complement the limestone look of the counters.

design details

• A happy blend of eclectic style and efficient design, the new bath mixes modern and traditional elements that will enable it to transcend decor trends for a long time to come.

• Warm touches like a natural grass-cloth cafe curtain panel and a wood-framed looking-glass lend earthy warmth.

• A towel warmer next to the tub injects an extra touch of luxury.

Opposite: Rasnick constructed a new second-floor addition to create a comfortable master suite. Right, top: The dimensions of the Japanese soaking tub were configured to eliminate tile cuts and accommodate specific tile runs. The tub tiles flow into the adjoining shower. Right, bottom: Matching dual vanities are topped by custom mirrors, which were hung at a slight tilt to reflect more elements in the room.

modern classic

Reality: The 80-year-old house that designer Steve Rasnick and his partner purchased in Charlotte, North Carolina, was in a great neighborhood, but its style was not in line with their contemporary sensibilities and it lacked a master suite altogether.

Dream: A spacious master suite including a bedroom with a window seat and fireplace adjoining a modern, two-person bath.

Making it manifest: In addition to renovating the entire house, Rasnick and his partner also constructed a new second-story addition atop the existing family room to create a brand-new 500-square-foot master suite, 210 feet of which is devoted to the bathroom. Here's what they did to shape the comfortable contemporary space:

1. The duo began with a contemporary view-through fireplace as a centerpiece. Stunningly simple and modern, the fireplace sets the minimalist tone for the spacious suite and provides a visual link between its two spaces.

2. The dividing wall that contains the fireplace was then crafted to multitask on each side. On the bedroom side, the fireplace surround of maple panel squares conceals a state-of-the-art audiovisual system. On the bath side, the gleaming glass of the fireplace and its golden fire are framed by a wall of 1-inch-square gray-veined Carrara marble mosaic tiles, which define the room with luxe simplicity.

3. To set a rich modern tone, they employed Carrara marble throughout the bath. Used prolifically in various forms on baseboards and backsplashes, in the shower, and, most magnificently, in the Japanese soaking tub, the marble was chosen for its durability and timelessness. As a slab, it also serves as a countertop, transitioning between two black granite sinks and floating hardwood cabinets.

4. They also balanced dedicated areas with shared ones. Two separate vanity cabinets flank a compact window seat composed of a fabric-covered cushion atop a drawer, which houses towels and toiletries and sits across from the separate shower stall.

design details:
• The plumbing fittings, originally designed in the 1950s by Danish designer Arne Jacobsen, remain a classic choice to this day.

• A water-efficient toilet and fittings and dimmers on lights make the space eco-friendly, and the fireplace takes the chill off cold days.

kitchen design checklist

Whether you're remodeling or starting from scratch, this kitchen design checklist will help you get the job done. Once it's completed, take it to a Certified Kitchen Designer (CKD), who can design a plan that will work for you. You'll be on your way to the kitchen of your dreams.

about the project

What is your budget? _____

When do you want to start the project?_____

When would you like to complete the project?_____

Will the kitchen be part of a new construction project or will it be a renovation of an existing home? _____

If it is a renovation, is it for resale or quality of life? _____

construction

Would you consider moving walls?_____

Would you consider an addition to the house?_____

Do you want to add or eliminate a window or skylight? _____

Do you need more than one kitchen?_____

Do you have any issues with heating or air conditioning? _____

Do you have any problems with insulation? _____

Are there any other considerations? _____

about you & the room

How long have you lived in the house? _____

How long do you envision staying? _____

Who is living/will live in the house and what are their approximate ages?
_____

Who works in the kitchen? How often? Are they left-handed or right-handed?
_____

What are their approximate heights? _____

Are there disabilities or allergies that should be considered in designing your new kitchen? _____

What do you most dislike about your current kitchen that should be avoided in the new one? _____

Is there anything about your current kitchen that you would like to incorporate into your new one? _____

Do you want to eat in the kitchen? Which meals? How many have to sit here?
_____

What's your preferred seating height (counter, bar or table)?
_____

Do you have pets? What type? _____

cooking

Who is the main cook? _____

Does more than one person cook simultaneously?_____

Are the cooks right- or left-handed?_____

How often are meals prepared from scratch?_____

How often are you home for lunch? _____

Do you make lunch for family members for work/school? How often? _____

For how many people? _____

Do you make family dinners regularly? How often? _____

For how many people? _____

storage & organization

How do you shop (weekly, daily, in bulk)? _____

Do you buy canned/boxed, prepared/frozen food or mostly fresh? _____

What kind of cooking do you do (stir-fry, casseroles, slow cooker, takeout, frozen/reheating, dessert)?_____

What are your spice storage and condiment storage requirements? _____

How many cookbooks will there be in the kitchen?_____

Do you prefer them to be visible? _____

Do you bake? If yes, how often?_____

Do you bake your own pastries?_____

Would you like any special display cabinets? _____

What would you like your cabinets to look like (painted, wood, traditional, contemporary)? _____

small appliances

Which ones need to be incorporated into the kitchen?

List items and approximate dimensions:

❏ Toaster

❏ Toaster oven

❏ Rice cooker

❏ Slow cooker

❏ Electric kettle

❏ Coffeemaker

❏ Pasta maker

❏ Bread maker

❏ Griddle

❏ Stand mixer

❏ Food processor

❏ Blender

❏ Panini grill

other activities

What activities other than conventional kitchen tasks are done in the kitchen (e.g., bill paying, computer games, TV, homework, crafts, laundry)?

_____

Do you need:
- ❏ Desk/message center
- ❏ Internet hub
- ❏ More than one phone line
- ❏ Fireplace
- ❏ TV/stereo
- ❏ Family-room seating

entertaining

How many people do you entertain? _____

Do you have large family gatherings? How often? _____

Do you host catered affairs? How often? _____

Do you do more formal or casual entertaining? _____

lighting

Do you prefer bright lighting? _____

Would you like the ability to dim lights? _____

Would you like to include decorative lighting? _____

Other comments about lighting: _____

_____

appliances

Will you buy new appliances or use existing ones? _____

Which from the list below do you want to include?
- ❏ Fridge
- ❏ Dishwasher
- ❏ Wall oven
- ❏ Cooktop
- ❏ Slide-in range
- ❏ Drop-in range
- ❏ Microwave (convection?) _____
- ❏ Warming drawer
- ❏ Steam oven
- ❏ Speed oven
- ❏ Built-in coffee/cappuccino maker
- ❏ Deep-fryer
- ❏ Beverage fridge
- ❏ Wine cooler
- ❏ Other _____

accessories

What cabinet accessories and/or features would you like?
- ❏ Tray/baking pan storage
- ❏ Pot drawers
- ❏ Spice storage (approx. how many jars?) _____
- ❏ Roll-out shelves
- ❏ Rotating corner shelves
- ❏ Pull-out towel rack or towel holders
- ❏ Recycling storage
- ❏ Pull-out/swing-out compost bin
- ❏ Wine storage (approx. how many bottles?) _____
- ❏ Carving knife storage
- ❏ Glass doors
- ❏ Cutlery dividers
- ❏ Utensil dividers
- ❏ Backsplash hanging rail
- ❏ Chopping block
- ❏ Swing-up food processor/stand mixer shelf
- ❏ Appliance garage
- ❏ Breadbox
- ❏ Pull-out baskets
- ❏ File drawers
- ❏ Pull-out keyboard shelf
- ❏ Broom cabinet fittings
- ❏ Stepladder
- ❏ Other _____

finishes

❏ Flooring material (hardwood, porcelain tile, cork, vinyl, linoleum, bamboo, etc.)

_____

❏ Countertop material (stone, quartz, stainless steel, laminate, etc.)

_____

❏ Backsplash (ceramic, glass tile, metal, etc.)

_____

❏ Cabinet material/finishes (stain, paint, distressed or antiqued finishes, etc.)

_____

❏ Other _____

fixtures, faucets, fittings & accessories

- ❏ Dish drainer (on the counter or in sink bowl?)_____
- ❏ Second/bar sink
- ❏ Faucets with sprayers
- ❏ Sink (stainless, single or double?)_____
- ❏ Sink colander
- ❏ Fitted cutting board
- ❏ Other _____

decorate

a room doesn't always require a major overhaul in order to get a lift. Slipcovers, a fresh coat of paint or a few new pillows are often all that's needed to breathe new life into a tired space. Whether you're starting from scratch or starting fresh with an established scheme, the homes on the following pages offer inspiration and ideas for every room—and for a variety of styles. All began with a clear stylistic point of view as well as a holistic plan, which establish a sense of continuity throughout and allow one room to flow into the other.

Right, top: Slipcovered chairs around a sturdy Crate & Barrel table soften the refined country home and are easy to clean. The pressed flowers were found at a flea market and framed. Right, bottom: A stone partition wall links the renovated kitchen to the living room. Opposite: The former pickled paneling was painted white to create a clean backdrop for crisp, transitional furnishings in the living room.

But all are also poised to evolve over time, with new layers that can inject new dimension as time goes on. And every scheme was also developed with an eye toward value and includes furnishings, accents and finishes that define style and boost comfort without incurring undue stress on the wallet.

cottage fresh

Reality: Jamie and Warren Stribling almost passed on purchasing their getaway home located in North Carolina's spectacular Cowee Ridge area. Structurally, the 2,000-square-foot home, built in 1983, was sound. But they weren't thrilled with the outdated kitchen and the overload of knotty pine paneling. Furthermore, despite the glorious surroundings, the house did little to bring the outdoors in. And it was contemporary in style—a total contrast to the charming cabin they'd envisioned. In the end, though, a gorgeous mountain vista won them over.

Dream: Initially, the Striblings considered a major remodel to create a cozier country style more suited to their tastes. But Craig Kettles, a Lakemont, Georgia–based interior designer, who'd recently masterminded a project for nearby in-laws, devised some innovative and less costly solutions: reconfiguring the kitchen, installing hardwood floors and updating surfaces. These minor renovations honored the existing architecture instead of competing with it. Then he followed up with furniture and accents to give the home the warmth and charm the owners desired.

Making it manifest: The designer enlisted help from Highlands, North Carolina, builder Dave Warth for the minor remodeling efforts. Then he took the following steps to reshape the house into an inviting getaway:

1. The dingy kitchen cabinets were ousted, making way for painted maple cabinets with lift-up doors. To replace a dowdy peninsula, the designer devised a fresh version with a stone front and waxed steel top. It now houses the range and has room for stools, allowing family and friends to hang out with the cook.

2. A massive hearth is the open plan's focal point, but bookcases with cabinets below dated it. So Kettles ripped out the built-ins to free wall space. Then, he mounted a steel mantel that mimics the kitchen's steel counter, linking the two architectural features and rooms together. An eye-popping sculpture crafted of organ pipes

Opposite (clockwise from top left): A new glass door creates an airier ambience inside the house. A new paneled ceiling lends extra stature to the bedroom. The new floor in the bath complements an original stone wall seen in the mirror. This page: Eco-friendly ipe wood, which resists rot and mold, replaced the old pressure treated lumber on the deck.

adds drama. Rustic chandeliers—in the sitting area and above the dining table—emphasize the lofty ceilings.

3. Kettles also paneled the bedroom ceilings and covered their floors with mountain-grass carpeting.

4. The baths were awarded new vanities atop cabinets painted a warm putty hue as well as stone-like ceramic tile on the floor.

5. The aging deck was revamped with sustainable ipe and sports an outdoor hearth. A cool steel railing frames the picture.

6. Finally, the whole interior was painted Benjamin Moore's Linen White to dispel gloom and magnify the light.

quick tricks

* **Bring nature in.** Mounting pressed flowers in matching frames and displaying them as a collection makes a strong yet accessible statement.

* **Dress your furniture.** Floor-length washable slipcovers with crisp kick pleats bring a touch of easy elegance to dining chairs.

* **Cute storage solution.** A boxy woven basket is the perfect place to stow rolled towels for easy access in a bath.

Right: Along the living room's bowed wall is a Knoll sofa adorned with tassels and finials. Lamps are antique mercury glass. Below: Vintage French portraits and landscapes mingle with a collection of cameos in a corner of the room where Singer placed a custom banquette.

easy elegance

Reality: Built in the 1950s, the home that designer Kate Singer shares with her husband and two daughters on Long Island Sound in New York, is modest in scale but full of interesting nooks and crannies. Its generous windows let in lots of light but were completely devoid of character.

Dream: An air of traditional elegance with a Continental twist and a touch of romance.

Making it manifest: As a designer, Singer travels frequently, often to Europe, and has picked up an extensive assortment of furniture and collectibles along the way, which reflect her preference for simple lines and traditional design and set the tone for the ambience in her own home. Here's how the designer approached cultivating the decor:

1. A muted seaside-inspired color scheme of sand, brown and pale blue sets a sophisticated tone.

2. Over the course of her many travel forays—mostly to various parts of Europe—Singer gathered an interesting combination of antiques and custom-made pieces, an impressive collection of art and accents, as well as a few bargain furnishings that she's refurbished to suit the decor, and used the furnishings throughout her home to create a sense of relaxed elegance.

3. By adding a desk and built-in upholstered corner banquette, like one in a French salon, to an awkward corner of the living room, the designer converted this unused zone into a cozy spot for taking tea or writing correspondence. The now comfortable area also gives her a place to display some of her French artwork and collectibles.

4. The brown tones that pepper the living room extend into the adjacent dining room, where walls are painted a deep cocoa hue. Though filled with formal antiques, the dining room is used almost every day. The color scheme also flows into the kitchen, which is warmed by the designer's collection of brown transferware and a window shade made of the curtain fabric used in the dining room.

5. Shades of gray and pale lilac dominate the master bedroom, giving it a peaceful air. Silk draperies and bedding enrich the room with a sense of quiet luxury.

quick tricks

* **Create displays in unexpected places.** You don't need to reserve artwork for formal areas, according to Singer. Think about displaying pieces in the bathroom, the kitchen— wherever you spend time and would enjoy something lovely to look at.

* **Mix it up.** Unless you're a purist, a collection doesn't have to contain items all of the same era or style, says Singer. She advises going for objects with a look that appeals to you, and not to be preoccupied with the pedigree.

* **Collect around an interest.** The designer's teenage daughter is an aspiring ballerina. She collects signed pointe shoes, which she grouped on a wall in her bedroom.

* **Group for effect.** Collections show to best advantage if they have a common thread—color, vintage, whatever. Consider collecting objects on your travels. A display of these collectibles, from seashells to expensive paintings, will evoke pleasant memories.

Casual matchstick blinds control privacy yet let in light as needed. A white slipcovered sofa gets pops of color with pillows and throws that tie into the upholstery fabric and accents in the room.

modern country

Reality: Years before interior designer and stylist Ingrid Leess moved into her New Canaan, Connecticut, home, its history as a charming family haven was well established. In the 1940s, its land was deeded to the housekeepers of a neighboring mansion, who built the comfy home for themselves and their six children. When Leess moved in nearly half a century later, little of the original structure had changed.

Dream: The designer wanted to maintain the integrity of its farmhouse style, but needed to expand the house. She also wanted to make the interior fresh with color and a personal mix of furnishings.

Making it manifest: Leess started by expanding the modular addition, placing careful attention on keeping the essence of its bucolic setting intact. Then she turned her focus to affordably decorating the rooms, which included establishing a base of furniture that she constantly updates with new accents and art. Here's how she developed her decor:

1. Since a majority of her pieces were either inherited from her Swedish grandmother or found at flea markets, they naturally reinforce the cozy, nostalgic spirit of the home. For accents, she looks everywhere from local church sales to the flea market in Paris.

2. The key to integrating her assorted treasures, says the designer, is all in the mix—combining new and old pieces in unexpected ways. An old scrubbed-pine coffee table adds personality to the family room, while her remarkable glass-bottle and ceramic collections create a striking tableau in the living room. For the latter, the designer installed basic shelving to contain her everchanging exhibits. At the moment she favors white pottery, but she collects things on a whim. Earlier it was silver trays, and in a couple of months it might be found objects.

3. As a long-time interiors stylist for shelter magazines, Leess knows all the tricks for keeping a home looking pictureperfect—and using slipcovers is top on her list.

4. Keeping her large furnishings—like puffy couches and roomy down-filled armchairs—in predominantly solid colors and a limited palette allows the designer to accent her rooms with changing color, pattern and texture combinations. Throughout, polka dots play off stripes, plaid shares space with damask, and sheepskin overlays sisal.

Opposite: By mounting long open shelves along one wall, the designer turned the empty space into a panorama of flea-market finds, hand-thrown ceramics and inexpensive pieces from IKEA. This page, clockwise from top: Random brown and white stripes bring energy to a wall in the foyer. In the bedroom, the headboard is made from two doors original to the house. The canopy is mounted directly to the ceiling. The designer painted the dark paneling throughout her home white to brighten the former dreary spaces.

quick tricks

* **Keep what's old, but don't hesitate to improve it.** Leess preserved the pine paneling in her living room, but painted it white.

* **Add interest with accents.** Leess likes to keep the colors of furnishings solid, then adds layers of pattern and texture with pillows, ceramics and artwork.

* **Take a chance with color.** Leess used chocolate-brown paint to add zing with a pattern of stripes on a wall next to her staircase.

* **Create double-duty built-ins.** With plywood and homemade foam cushions, Leess constructed window seats in her bedroom. She put a skirt on them to create extra storage below.

* **Add open shelves.** The ones in her bedroom are made with planks from The Home Depot and supported by brackets from IKEA. They allow for a ton of display and storage options.

acknowledgments

It may take a village to raise a child, but it also takes one to create a book—and this one was no exception. Several manufacturers, retailers, designers and experts offered support with products, materials, services, advice and ideas on several of my own projects, which are featured in this book. Among them are Benjamin Moore, Bourgeoise3D, Brookhaven/Wood-Mode, Budget Blinds, California Closets, Cosentino/Silestone, Country Floors, Elkay, IKEA, Secoda Carpentry and Sherwin-Williams, along with all of the pros on their teams who helped me—and I would like to thank them all for their generosity and professionalism. I called upon several experts for insight and expertise in the development of my projects—and all also deserve my thanks. They include Atsushi Shono, Katherine Lewis, Kathleen Cox and Mayank Barjatya. Special thanks also go to my kitchen designer, Dave Burcher of Inhouse Kitchen Bath Home, and my contractor, John Loffredo of Sure Fit Designs, who made sure everything went right with the toughest parts of my efforts. I would also like to thank the many public relations professionals who eased the access to many of the sources I relied upon to create so much of the content of this book. While they're too numerous to mention, their usually unsung work is quietly woven into the fabric of these pages—and I am indebted and grateful to them all. I would also like to thank my publisher, Dorothée Walliser, and her associate, Barbara Slavin, for their continuous and gracious support—this book would not have happened without them. Dorothée also enlisted two of the industry's best art directors, Keith D'Mello and Jeff Felmus, as the designers of this book—and I am grateful to both of them for making *The Happy Home Project* beautiful. My gratitude also goes to photographer Paul Whicheloe, who photographed all of the rooms in my own home, as well as a few of its nooks and crannies, and completed every shot on my lengthy list on a late fall day with limited sun. Of course, my family, friends and extended family of industry friends are also part of the community that contributed to the making of this book—and my very special thanks go to all of them, too!

sources

architects & designers

C Designs (Craig Kettles)
c-designs.biz
Exquisite Kitchen Design (Mikal Otten)
myekdesign.com
Green Couch
greencouch.com
Ingrid Leess Design
ILeess@aol.com
J. Hurst & Associates
jhurstassociates.com
Jean Stoffer Design
jeanstofferdesign.com
John Clagett Architect
jclagettl@verizon.net
Kate Singer Home
katesingerhome.com
Lifescape Associates (Mike Ransom)
lifescapeassociates.com
Steven Rasnick Interior Design
stevenrasnickinteriordesign.com
Sure Fit Designs
jsfdl@aol.com

experts

Mayank Barjatya
vastuworld.com
Kathleen Cox
vastuliving.com
Katherine Lewis
Harmony and Balance
harmonyandbalance.com
Sonu Mathew
Livingcolorwithsonu.com
Atsushi Shono
Feng Shui Stones
Fengshui-stones.com;
fengshui@cybercap

manufacturers & retailers

Adrienne Neff
adrienneneff.com
Angie's List
Angieslist.com
Anthropologie
anthropologie.com
Art.com
art.com
Art We Love
artwelove.com
Benjamin Moore
benjaminmoore.com
Bona
bona.com
Bourgeoisie3D
bourgeoisie3d.com

Budget Blinds
budgetblinds.com
California Closets
californiaclosets.com
CertaPro
certapro.com
Chelsea Frames
chelseaframes.com
Coco-Mat
coco-mat.com
Cosentino
cosentinonorthamerica.com
Country Floors
countryfloors.com
C.R. Laine Furniture
crlaine.com
Decorator's Best
decoratorsbest.com
DiggersList
diggerslist.com
Elfa
elfa.com
Elkay
elkay.com
The Future Perfect
thefutureperfect.com
Gaggenau
gaggenau.com
Garnet Hill
garnethill.com
Gotham Organizers
gothamorganizers.com
Graham & Brown
grahambrown.com
Hickory Chair
hickorychair.com
IKEA
ikea.com
Inhouse Kitchen Bath Home Design
inhousekbh.com
Jasco Chemical Corp.
jasco-help.com
Kincaid Furniture
kincaidfurniture.com
Lands' End
landsend.com
Larson Juhl
larsonjuhl.com
Lifekind
lifekind.com
Lutron Electronics
lutron.com
Mattress Safe
mattresssafe.com
Organic Mattresses Inc.
omimattress.com
NaturaWorld
naturaworld.com
Secoda Carpentry
secoda89@yahoo.com
Serena & Lily
serenaandlily.com

ServiceMagic
servicemagic.com
Sherwin-Williams
sherwin-williams.com
Silestone
silestoneusa.com
3-M
3m.com
Wallpaper Collective
wallpapercollective.com
Walnut Wallpaper
walnutwallpaper.com
Wood-Mode
wood-mode.com
Yolo Colorhouse
yolocolorhouse.com
York Wallcoverings
yorkwall.com

associations & organizations

Alliance for Climate Protection
climateprotect.org
Alliance to Save Energy
ase.org
American Home Furnishings Alliance
ahfa.us; Sustainablebydesign.us
American Lung Association
lungusa.org
American Society of Interior Designers in partnership with the U.S. Green Building Council
greenhomeguide.org
American Solar Energy Society
ases.org
American Wind Energy Association
awea.org
Association of Home Appliance Manufacturers
aham.org
Asthma and Allergy Foundation of America
aafa.org
Better Sleep Council
bettersleep.org
Database of State Incentives for Renewables & Efficiency
dsireusa.org
Department of Energy
doe.gov
Earth Easy
eartheasy.com
Efficient Products
efficientproducts.org

Energy Star program
energystar.gov
Federal Trade Commission
ftc.gov
Forest Stewardship Council
fsc-info.org
General Electric
gelighting.com
Get Energy Active
getenergyactive.org
Greenguard Environmental Institute
greenguard.org
Habitat for Humanity
Habitatforhumanity.org
Health House
healthhouse.org
Home Safety Council
homesafetycouncil.org
Housing Works
housingworks.org
International Feng Shui Association
intfsa.org
Kitchen Cabinet Manufacturers Association
greencabinetsource.org
National Association of Home Builders
nahb.org
National Association of the Remodeling Industry
nariremodelers.com;
greenremodeling.org
The National Fenestration Rating Council
nfrc.org
National Guild of Professional Paper Hangers
ngpp.org
National Kitchen & Bath Association
nkba.org
Natural Resources Defense Council
nrdc.org
Society of American Florists
safnow.org
Sustainable Furnishings Council
sustainblefurnishings.org
Sustainable Forestry Initiative, Inc.
sfiprogram.org
U.S. Green Building Council
usgbc.org

Wallcoverings Association
wallcoverings.org
Water Sense program
epa.gov/watersense
Water Use It Wisely
wateruseitwisely.com
World Floor Covering Association
wfca.org

bibliography

A Perfect Mess
(Little Brown),
Eric Abrahamson and
David Freedman

Architect's Guide to Feng Shui
(Architectural Press),
Cate Bramble

Even the Stars Look Lonesome (Random House), Maya Angelou

Feng Shui: The Chinese Art of Placement
(Penguin),
Sarah Rossbach

House Thinking
(Harper Collins),
Winifred Gallagher

The Poetics of Space
(Beacon Press),
Gaston Bachelard

The Wabi-Sabi House
(Clarkson Potter),
Robyn Griggs Lawrence

27 Things to Feng Shui Your Home
(Trade Paper Press),
Tisha Morris

Vastu: Transcendental Home Design in Harmony with Nature (Gibbs Smith),
Sherri Silverman

Vastu Living
(HarperCollins),
Kathleen Cox